Children of Ch

Children of Chernobyl

The Human Cost of the World's Worst Nuclear Disaster

Adi Roche

Fount
An Imprint of HarperCollins*Publishers*

Fount Paperbacks is an Imprint of
HarperCollins *Religious*
Part of HarperCollins *Publishers*
77–85 Fulham Palace Road, London W6 8JB

First published in Great Britain
in 1996 by Fount Paperbacks

5   7   9   10   8   6   4

A catalogue record for this book is
available from the British Library

0 00 627927-9

Printed and bound in Great Britain by
Caledonian International Book Manufacturing Ltd, Glasgow G64

This book is dedicated to the courage
and strength of seven-year-old
Evgeniya Nesterenko
1987–1995

Contents

Acknowledgements

The events in this book began in 1991 with an SOS fax appeal from doctors in the affected regions seeking help for their children. My first visit to Chernobyl was in 1992. I witnessed at first hand the consequences of the tragedy, and the seed of an idea for a documentary was planted in my mind. The next visit was in the company of an Irish film crew in April 1993. Other visits were made to lay the ground-work for our Humanitarian Aid programme. Accompanied by two Icelandic film crews, I made a dramatic return on 1st January 1995 for the first ever emergency air lift from the Chernobyl area of Belarus to the West. Two later visits were made in the Spring and the Autumn of 1995, when I returned with two aid convoys.

Top of my list of acknowledgements is my husband, Seán Dunne, who missed Christmas, the New Year and numerous other special occasions because I was away or working around the clock in the office. Seán, for all those times you have had to spend alone, especially the cold nights, I say a massive 'thank you'. You always gave me great encouragement, particularly when I was tired and had lost heart in my ability to write.

'Thanks' to all my friends who have not seen me for many months (in some cases even years!) and have still remained my friends. Special thanks to the other members of the 'Holy Trinity', Liz and Maureen, who have carried me through many crises. They sustained me in my darkest moments of self-doubt and listened to endless monologues about the trials and tribulations associated with my work. Also to the other members of 'The Bubbles', four women friends who together make up one hell of a singing group, I say 'sorry' for missing all those nights of rehearsals over the years.

Many people have passed through the Irish CND office who

deserve mention: my old pal and loyal worker Norrie McGregor; Mary Murray of Ogra Chorcai for being one of the key initiators of the Chernobyl Children's Project; Eamonn Hodnett and Colin Carroll, who spent long hours running off early drafts of this book; Barbara Deasy for her tireless work and support on everything; and those who are still there, Fleur and Lydia Dixon, Emer O'Neill and Fiona Corcoran. Special thanks to Eoin Dinan for his endless help throughout my work over the past 16 years. He has been exceptional also in his boundless support for the work on Chernobyl, and when Sasha and Vitaly were in Crumlin Hospital he spent countless hours looking after the children and their mothers. For the medical section of the book, I thank doctors Sean and Mary Dunphy for their great help and patience. Thanks too to Jonathon Williams, my book agent, for his gentle kindness and assistance, and thanks to Giles Semper of HarperCollins for having the faith in me to write this book.

Ann Norman and Mary Aherne must be given mention for travelling with me around the highways and byways of Ireland in all kinds of weather and at all hours of the day and night. I'm sure they cursed me many times for ever involving them in Chernobyl, especially on nights like that one down in Kenmare when we ran out of petrol at 1 a.m. and had no place to go until we flagged down a squad car! We have travelled endless hours together and every one of them was full of laughs and jokes, with the odd smattering of 'serious' stuff! I think you two are brill!

The poems interspersed throughout this book come from the literary talents of a dear old friend and supporter, Greg Delanty, who was inspired to write these poems as a result of hearing the stories of the people and seeing the documentary. For me, the poems add a very special dimension, not only because they are exceptionally good but because they capture what has been lost.

Thanks to everyone in the DreamChaser Production Company – the crew, Ali, Dónal, Dan, Isobel, Liam and Jerry, and particularly to Ned O'Hanlon for taking such a risk in putting up the money for the documentary. Folks, there will always be a huge place in my heart for you all.

It isn't often that people lavish praise on their governments, but I'm happy to say that I can and I do: particularly our Minister for the Environment (formerly Minister for Health), Brendan

Acknowledgements

Howlin, and his assistant, Anne Byrne; the Minister for Foreign Affairs, Dick Spring, and his staff; the Minister for Defence and the Marine, Hugh Coveney; the Minister for Health, Michael Noonan; and the Minister for Arts, Culture and the Gaeltacht, Michael D. Higgins.

Finally, thanks to the people of Chernobyl for allowing me to become part of their story. They deserve credit for their incredible courage and strength of mind and heart, and for taking such personal risks to talk to me so that their silence would finally be broken.

Adi Roche
Director, Chernobyl Children's Project

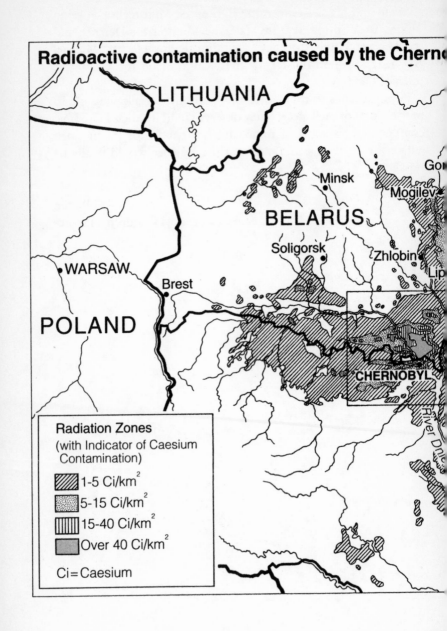

Radioactive contamination caused by the Chern[o...]

LITHUANIA

BELARUS

Minsk

Go[...]

Mogilev

Soligorsk

Zhlobin

Lip[...]

WARSAW

Brest

POLAND

CHERNOBYL

River Dni[...]

Radiation Zones
(with Indicator of Caesium Contamination)

1-5 Ci/km^2

5-15 Ci/km^2

15-40 Ci/km^2

Over 40 Ci/km^2

Ci = Caesium

losion

MOSCOW•

0 _____ 200
kilometres

RUSSIAN
FEDERATION

Klintsy
ovozybkov

Gomel

Rechitsa

River Dnieper

Mozyr

Tulgovichi Khoniki
Strelichevi
Novelselki Mikulvichi
Bragin

CHERNOBYL

KRAINE

Belarussians after Chernobyl

As I join the women on the night porch
seesawing their confab back and forth
on chatting rockers, I think of you

or rather how I don't want to think of
what's happened to you as hurricane lamps
fan us with gentle light and gentler darkness

and the background crickets support us with
their singing wings that I can't do justice to,
nor understand, just as I can't the unknown

singing bird in the darkness of unknown trees,
nor the background soprano sopranoing,
except I've always been silently thankful

that I never understood Puccini's language,
allowing the words to become wordless music.
And now more than ever I want handicapped

words to turn into such music that will recreate
a miraculous humdrum night such as ours
for you: with voices telling unbelievable tales;

with hurricane lamps, crickets, birds and trees
and one woman watering the blossoming vincas
while the other says it's best to water at night;

and how utterly I do not understand this
or anything of what shattered the glass of
your erstwhile ordinary days and nights.
   Greg Delanty

Introduction

The splitting of the atom has changed everything except our way of thinking and thus we drift towards unparalleled catastrophe. *Albert Einstein*

Head against the fogged-up window which couldn't be opened because of the fear of radiation dust; numbed, sweating, terrified underneath my radiation protection suit, I began to question my very sanity. What in the hell was I doing in the world's most radioactive environment? Inner cries of 'Help!' rushed to the surface. I felt engulfed by a strong sense of panic. I couldn't breathe. My heart raced and felt as if it might burst. I looked at the geiger counter in my hand and – my God! – I saw the needle rise beyond what it was capable of registering. My fear was over-whelming. Feelings of sinking deep into a black hole rushed forth like a torrent of evil. I screamed silently. I was in my own private world of terror. I had just entered 'Death Valley', the exclusion zone surrounding Chernobyl.

What had brought me here was 16 years of working for peace and justice. Working for a world which could embrace the dreams and visions of our children, encompassing the needs and aspirations of us all. A belief that I could help to change the minds and hearts of others. A belief in the sanctity of life and in the holiness of the earth. My mind was grappling with the ethos of what had carried me to Chernobyl, but the fear was rising high. My words of 'wisdom' began to dim and fail me in this place of strange evil. As our van raced along the dusty, radioactive roads, I felt chilled to my very marrow, under armed escort, facing the reality of man's destructive capabilities. The strangeness of our 'escorts' added to my unease. Men whose sole function was to guard the exclusion zone so that no one could now enter it.

1

Looking at my companions – an Irish film crew sent with the task of filming a documentary which would tell the world the truth about the aftermath of the Chernobyl accident – I felt ill with the weight of responsibility. The bravery we had felt earlier had evaporated. Each of us was now afraid to divulge our inner horror. We stayed locked in our private worlds. I felt as if I was in a state of suspension between two worlds. My mother's promise to light a church candle daily failed to ease me. Frantically my mind fled into its darkest recesses to find something to sustain me. Images of my parents and closest ones flashed in and out. Prayers and words of laughter squeezed their way in between the blackness. With all of this rush of emotion my personal story of Chernobyl unfolded.

The strength and optimism of the Belarussian poet Ouladzimir Dubovka came to mind and encouraged me:

Oh Belarus, my wild rose,
A green leaf, a red flower
Neither whirlwind will ever bind you
Nor Chernobyl will ever cover.

Today Chernobyl is beating in the hearts of all Belarussians. It beats with radioactive particles registered in geiger counters, in their fields, streets, cities and towns. It is in the deceivingly tranquil beauty of the forests, rivers and streams that no one may now enter. As I looked around the lifeless fields, I thought of the despair of the peasant farmer who was now unable to cultivate the land on which his ancestors had grown crops for centuries. I thought of the grief and helplessness of a mother watching her children die. Driving through deserted villages, I thought of the silent sorrow of old people who had to leave forever the native places they held sacred, places where they had spent their lives and where they left the graves of their loved ones.

The prophetic words of Albert Einstein rolled around my head with the sudden recognition that he had foreseen the nightmare which we had just entered. Locked in this unreal yet real world, we drove on into what had become a living hell.

1
Life-changing times

M Y LIFE UNTIL 1978 was full of ordinary, regular events, but 27th March 1979 changed all that. The accident at the Three Mile Island nuclear plant near Harrisburg, Pennsylvania brought with it personal fears for my brother Dónal and his family who were living near the plant. I remember asking, 'What is nuclear power?' I soon discovered that we were about to have a nuclear power plant built by the Irish government at a beautiful place called Carnsore Point in County Wexford. Out of curiosity I went along to the first anti-nuclear rally against the building of the plant, and this proved to be a pivotal episode which would change the direction of my life.

The rally gave me a glimpse of Ireland's alternative people. That's putting it mildly! I had to sometimes remind myself to stop staring at people who could only be described as the wild and wonderful! I was at various times shocked and somewhat amazed by the diversity of people and lifestyles. I encountered my first vegetarians, hells angels and nudists, along with people committed to non-violence, indigenous people's rights and alternative energy. Basically it was a whole new world of people to me.

I attended many workshops (most of which I didn't understand!) and encountered political viewpoints that were alien to my world. Listening to the founder of the Green Party, Petra Kelly, laid the seeds of my personal transformation. Petra enraptured and captured me with her energy, eloquence, courage and love for the planet. She spoke about the earth with such creativity that she touched a chord in my soul that was waiting to be awakened and given life. So much of what Petra spoke about that day and in subsequent meetings echoed what was dormant in my own heart.

Sitting in this wonderful spot on the east coast of Ireland along with 20,000 others and listening to Irish music heroes Christy Moore and Paul Brady, I began to feel a part of something incredibly powerful. Unconsciously a new life pathway was being woven by me and for me.

Until now, I had worked for Ireland's national airline, Aer Lingus, and bit by precious bit I became more drawn to wanting to work on peace and environmental issues. My heart was increasingly whispering to me to take stock of my life and look at the possibility of new directions. During this period I had become a member of Friends of the Earth and had started to campaign against the building of the reactor. This campaign had immense popular support and eventually the government had to concede that it had lost the pro-nuclear battle, and it not only shelved the plans for the reactor but also abandoned uranium mining projects throughout the country. Our lobbying and campaigning was so effective that we virtually succeeded in getting the government to reverse its decision, and I can safely say that as a result of the education work from the late seventies we in Ireland now have a healthy allergy to anything nuclear! With these two major successes ringing in our ears, we became part of the Campaign for Nuclear Disarmament, with a view to ridding the world of nuclear weapons.

At the height of the Cold War I resigned my airline position to become the full-time voluntary worker for CND in Ireland. I devised and implemented a 'Peace Education Programme' for young people in response to their palpable fears of environmental disaster and the threat of nuclear war. This work, which I initiated in 1982, is still a very significant part of my life. In a school curriculum which is mainly academic and geared towards intense learning, I felt it of the upmost importance to introduce something new and fresh which would look towards the development of a different kind of 'learning', one which would encourage creativity and the exploration of the 'wider world', something that would promote self-education and an awareness that would also nurture the values of co-operation, participation and dialogue. These positive qualities could then be reflected not only in the classroom but would also permeate out into the community and society at large.

During the bleakest moments of the 1980s the spirit, energy

and enthusiasm of the young people I was working with helped to carry me through to better times.

Many events and people have influenced and sustained me over the years. I remember in 1982 being among a rally of one million people in New York, along with my husband, as part of the Irish delegation attending the UN as observers to the Second Special Session on Disarmament. Going backstage and meeting people like Joan Baez, a woman whom I admire greatly, heightened my excitement. Meeting my other heroes in New York, such as Bruce Kent, the British Labour MP Bob Cryer and Coretta Scott-King, was a wonderful experience. My husband, Seán, had the honour of addressing the crowd of one million, along with a Hopi Elder whose words of truth I recall, particularly when the planet screams in pain and torment:

> *Mother Earth is only one being*
> *And we, the children of all Nations*
> *Must learn to protect her*
> *And all living things*
> *To help to hold the world in balance.*

It is not easy to maintain that balance, and part of what I try to do in the schools is to encourage students to work on inner balance, a peace which ultimately radiates out to the wider world community. I encourage a belief that the power of our own love can overcome the love of power. I try to instil a belief in the holiness of the earth and the sanctity of all life. To cope with the lunacy of the world we live in, a lot of our work involves the analysis of world problems and looking at and learning from individuals and groups of people who have helped to change the world through the courage of their convictions.

This 'mentor/model' role includes bringing into the classroom the stories of Gandhi, Martin Luther King, Petra Kelly, Seán MacBride and others. Some of the role models come right into the classroom! Over the years I have brought to hundreds of classrooms women from the Greenham Common peace camp, crews from visiting Greenpeace ships, Bruce Kent from British CND, and Commander Robert Green (Rtd.) of the World Court Project. All these people and many others have come and shared their experiences and moments of transformation with the students and have acted as a major force in creating whole generations of young people with a burning desire and passion for the earth.

In more recent times I have seen the significance of such education translate into political change. In the European elections in the spring of 1994, for example, we saw two Greens in the Leinster constituency elected to the European Parliament for the first time. All over the country the Greens have been slowly but surely getting elected at local government level. On the doorstep I have been told that many of the people voting Green are doing so because of their concern for environmental issues, particularly nuclear issues, and a lot of the education of the younger voters relates back to what they heard and experienced in the classroom.

I feel saddened when I think about the state of the world that our children will inherit. To help ensure that their legacy is protected, I try to encourage them to constantly celebrate the gift of the earth. In the classroom we often take just 30 seconds 'time out' to sit back, close our eyes, and think of some place special that we like. In this half-minute the children find their place of comfort and beauty and learn to respect and honour it.

I love talking to primary school children because they get as enthusiastic as I do about understanding the Gaia theory, named after the Greek goddess of the earth. This is the theory of the scientist Dr James Lovelock, who believes that our planet itself is a living, self-sustaining entity and that we are just another interconnected part of the life-cycle. It always leads to a lively discussion on what the American Indians called the 'web of life'. The children draw it and are very quick to point out to me that if we damage the strands of the web we damage ourselves ultimately.

I always encourage the children to look back and read the words written by the first astronauts who went into space, and to try and share some of the magic these men experienced when they looked down at this big, blue, beautiful planet with no frontiers. What they saw in the darkness of space was the vivid colour and movement of a living thing. This always leads on to talking about the miracle of life on earth, and how we could have been just another barren planet in the galaxy of the Milky Way, had it not been for the ozone layer which has wrapped us up and swathed us from the dangers of the ultra-violet rays of the sun.

Describing how life was able to evolve over billions of years invariably gets a few gasps of excitement, and the children are thrilled no end as they learn to discover the beauty of their home. Not only do we look at the gift of our habitat and our responsibility for ensuring its survival, but we also take stock and wonder at the uniqueness of our own species. While the planet has been busy evolving over billions of years, so have we! I always love to talk with children about the miracle of the human species, in which there are no two people the same! Out of all the billions of humans on the earth, we are all unique, different and special. The sense of 'specialness' and 'giftedness', along with evoking the notion that they have been loved from before the beginning, helps to lay strong foundations of respect for themselves, for one another and for the planet.

We often move the discussions on to trying to learn about why mankind has ended up being so disconnected from this wonderful creation, and this means we talk about what we can learn from other indigenous peoples, whose way of being with the earth is different to ours in one fundamental respect. It has got to do with how we perceive the earth itself. Our way is about 'ownership', thinking that we can destroy the earth and expect it to be able to replenish and recover. The Native American Indian ethos embraces a much more holistic belief that we are the caretakers, the nurturers of the earth of our children and our children's children. My own love of life and all creation is essential to my work in schools, and I suppose you could say that I am an eternal optimist! I always try to see good and to work as much as possible on the positive. I think I can honestly say that I am in 'passion' and 'compassion' with the earth.

When discussing war in school, students sometimes express strong feelings that we cannot alter human nature, which they perceive to be a genetically violent one. Looking around at the state of our warring world, I can fully sympathize with that feeling and conclusion. But I take great delight in introducing the UNESCO 'Statement on Violence' which says very clearly, among other things, that 'war is not a biological necessity'. So if war is a learned behaviour, what's to stop us from unlearning it?! There is absolutely no insurmountable obstacle to the abolition of war and violence, so we can free ourselves from the bondage of biological pessimism and empower each other with confidence to transform towards the mind of peace. Just as wars begin in the minds of men, so also can peace begin in all our minds. As a species that has developed war, so too are we capable of inventing peace. And with this a whole new debate emerges.

All these discussions lead to a greater understanding that we do not have to be rendered helpless or powerless. Our children are the hope for the future, and the more involved they feel in their world, the better off we shall all be. Providing ourselves as well as our children with positive visions of the future of life, with all the beauty and diversity of nature, is fundamental to ensuring a constant rising force for genuine change.

So when I feel that the unfairness of the world is getting a little bit overwhelming, I go to a school, and while I come home tired, there is a part of me that has been invigorated and refreshed, ready to 'save the world' again tomorrow!

Looking back and reflecting on what has motivated and sustained me to continue in what could be perceived as 'despair work', I think the answer may lie with the importance which my parents gave to moral responsibility, along with a keen sense of justice. They were both active in Irish political life and in our local community. They had a particular concern for the plight of the Irish Travellers and were instrumental in supporting travelling families around our local town of Clonmel in County Tipperary. Both often spoke of the importance of conscience and the need for each of us to accept our role in ensuring that the world became a better and more equal place. My upbringing had a strong religiousness to it without being overbearing. So really its not too surprising that I have ended up in the business of 'caring for creation', considering the seeds of concern for the protection of the earth and all species that were planted throughout the years of my youth.

Even going back to before the influence of my parents, I honestly believe that I have been deeply affected by my maternal and paternal grandmothers, all unknown to them. They were sowing the seeds in my young receptive mind for the Project to which I became dedicated. My sister and brothers and I spent long summer holidays with our maternal granny and we loved her. She was petite and the soul of kindness. She never spoke unkindly about anybody and loved helping those who were not so well off.

She often reminisced about her departed husband, Con. He had been the head-teacher of the local school, and we children loved hearing about him and his concern for all his pupils. He was obviously a dedicated teacher and took particular interest in the less well-off pupils, whom he brought in to school on Saturdays to give them that little bit of extra tuition to help prepare them for a better future. She was very proud of the achievements of his past pupils. Every summer, these boys, now successful men on holiday from their various positions, called to see Granny and reminisced and chatted with her about her beloved Con. He had even supplied them with books, paid for out of his own pocket, to help them escape from the drudgery of being 'hewers of wood and drawers of water'. I loved listening to all this and often thought that generosity surely had its own reward.

When Granny herself, who lived to be 84, started to deteriorate, we were all very sad, but my Auntie Mary, who lived near her, together with her husband and family, surrounded her with love and care, just as she herself had done for everyone.

My paternal grandmother often came to our house. We loved her too, but in a different way. She was tall and most of her reminiscences were about the injustices her farming family had endured during the Land War of the nineteenth century, when they were forced to leave their large home farm in Mount North for a smaller farm in Doneraile, County Cork, all because her grandfather had voted for a Catholic magistrate. This change of lifestyle, however, did not prevent the family from helping stricken victims of the Great Famine in the 1840s. According to her, they set up a soup kitchen at the gate, and different members of the family helped in the distribution of food. My sister and I often spoke of hoping for a chance to help others too. Our paternal grandfather came of farming stock and set up an excellent business in Doneraile. He was an active member of the local St Vincent de Paul Society. My Dad remembers how charitable he was and how during World War II he often delivered presents of tea and sugar, both of which were rationed, to his St Vincent de Paul 'clients'.

Last year I finally recognized that there was another significant experience that left me profoundly changed and mapped the direction into which I would eventually travel. I had been born and reared with a neighbour's child called Ann Condon. We lived in each other's pockets, so to speak, from the time we could walk and talk. All of the major things that are significant in growing up we did simultaneously, such as making our Holy Communion and Confirmation. We even met and fell in love with young lads together. We shared the same desk in school. All this was shattered when we entered our final year in school and Ann was diagnosed as having leukaemia. We didn't know what that was until we looked up a home medical journal and both learned that her days were numbered.

When we parted and she was taken to hospital in Dublin, we wrote steadfastly to each other. Our letters were always full of jokes and fun, never addressing our fears of death – a death which was painful and full of unanswered questions. I remember walking around her coffin in the church, walking after it into the grave-yard, watching it being lowered down and covered forever by the dark earth. I thought my heart would break and wanted nothing better than to die myself. In the years since her death, I have often sensed her presence and protection in my life, and I acknowledge now that unconsciously all my years of work for a better world are dedicated in her honour.

2

The monster that has never been tamed

T HE WORLD'S WORST nuclear accident happened on 26th April 1986 at the Chernobyl nuclear power station in northern Ukraine: 190 tons of highly radioactive uranium and graphite were expelled into the atmosphere. The result was an international ecological calamity on an extreme scale, and it has turned out to be a grave disaster and sorrow for the people of Belarus, western Russia and northern Ukraine. According to some estimates, at least 9 million people have been affected directly or indirectly.

The radioactive plume from the burning reactor moved north and then west and on into Poland and Sweden, where it was first detected, taking with it radioactive Iodine 131, over millions of unsuspecting people. Caesium and Strontium, which are longer-living isotopes, were dispersed over a vast area of 160,000 square kilometres. A UN report (September 1995) estimates that an area the size of England, Wales and Northern Ireland combined has been contaminated.

Almost 2,200,000 Belarussian people have been subjected to permanent radioactive contamination of varying density. Of the country's prime farmland and forest, 25% has become nuclear wasteland. Dozens of villages and towns have ceased to exist. New spots of radioactive contamination are still being discovered. Areas that were clean yesterday are contaminated today. Radionuclides are being detected in people in uncontaminated zones. Only 1% of their land remains uncontaminated, so there is little or no access to 'clean food'. Of the 100 million curies released into the atmosphere from Chernobyl, over 70% fell on to the population of Belarus, and as a result over 800,000 children in Belarus and a further 380,000 Ukrainian children are at high risk of contracting cancer or leukaemia. The entire territory of Belarus has become a zone of international ecological disaster. At the United Nations Belarussian scientists have declared this to be the greatest environmental disaster in the history of humanity.

The consequences of the disaster have turned out to be much larger and more serious than was predicted by many, including prominent scientists and experts. This is a tragedy of planetary proportions. Plutonium has spread much further than the 30-kilometre exclusion zone. In post-mortem examinations, serious traces of radioactivity were found in people who lived several hundred kilometres from Chernobyl. In the Gomel region of Belarus and the Bryansk region of Russia, changes have been found in chromosome analysis. These changes could only result from exposure to powerful radiation doses – 1,000 rads or more, which is a result of plutonium fission, according to Soviet scientist Andrei Vorobyov, Director of the All-Union Hematological Scientific Centre. Vorobyov also revealed in an article printed in the *Moscow News* in August 1991 that radiation doses which had been published were incorrect and understated by several times.

Owing to the doses of external and internal irradiation received from short-lived radionuclides and being constantly exposed to long-lived radionuclides, the people in the affected areas have received the highest-known exposure in the history of the atomic age. No people have ever before been continuously exposed to long-lived, man-made radiation. *The people of Chernobyl were exposed to radioactivity 90 times greater than that from the explosion of the Hiroshima atomic bomb.*

The fears for the future of the nuclear industry which Chernobyl caused in the minds of its advocates are no justification for the lack of information available to the world community about the true scale of the disaster. This lack merely holds back the development of international solidarity and the flow of voluntary assistance to the victims.

The holding back of information was facilitated by the lack of preparedness of many Western governments. The inconsistencies in their actions are chilling. In West Germany many restrictions were placed on the movement of children and on the consumption of dairy products. But in many other countries people were told that there was nothing to worry about. In Ireland people were scared, did not know what to do and had no one to turn to until Irish CND along with the Irish Medical Campaign for the Prevention of Nuclear War, in response to hundreds of pleas for advice and help, operated a 24-hour 'information hotline'. At the time people were calling us 'alarmists'. Unfortunately, time has proved that we were anything but.

Much confusion arose over 'acceptable' levels of radiation, which varied from country to country. In Ireland the government was far more lax than that of West Germany, even though the levels of radiation we received were practically the same. The difficulty of getting adequate information, not only in the immediate aftermath of the accident but also in the following years, has concerned me deeply. Even those of us in the environmental and anti-nuclear movements did little work on the aftermath of Chernobyl for the first five years, as if somehow we too had been lulled into a false belief that everything was miraculously all right. Or perhaps we had so much madness to cope with in trying to keep the superpowers from nuclear annihilation that we had our hands full! Somewhere along the line we had also been duped by the clever cover-up created by the former USSR. It was only in 1991, five years after the accident, that I started to spend some time trying to uncover the reason for such a void in information and general lack of response. I was shocked by what I discovered to be a large part of the answer.

Thanks to the work of a very courageous Ukrainian journalist, Alla Yaroshinskaya, we now know about the 40 secret Protocols signed by the Politburo. The jigsaw puzzle surrounding the whole question of access to information began to fall in to place. The Protocols permitted a scandalous censorship and control over the media and thereby stopped the flow of information to the rest of the world. The calculated manner in which the former USSR covered up the true scale of the accident horrifies me.

The Protocols controlled the information given to the International Atomic Energy Agency (IAEA) and 'to certain leaders of capitalist countries'. The World Health Organisation (WHO) has based its figures and findings on the information given to the IAEA, which we now know were monitored and very selective. Deliberate 'misinformation' given to the West has ensured that the real consequences of the accident remained secret until recent times. It reminds me of the aftermath of the nuclear bombs being dropped on Hiroshima and Nagasaki in 1945, and how the consequences were kept a military secret for a decade. It is chilling to think that in this modern age of information it appears that very little has changed when the 'powers that be' do not want us to know something.

When I started to research the consequences of the accident, I never ceased to be amazed at how effective were the secrecy and misinformation of the USSR. Not only was everything kept secret, but because of inadequate diplomatic efforts to disseminate information about the true scale of the disaster to the international community, the aid response from the West has been abysmal. It is difficult to say why there was such secrecy and lack of truth. Sometimes I wonder whether the deception was caused by the secrecy, or whether the secrecy was the result of the deception. Either way, the response by the USSR was inhuman. I use the word 'inhuman' with great care.

The Soviet Union's long-standing obsessive secrecy about nuclear affairs is despicable and shows an appalling lack of respect for the dangers bound up in the atom. The cold, stark reality of the decisions taken and enshrined in the Protocols has had very wide and devastating significance. In Protocol Number 9, for example, the authorities gave themselves permission to increase and change the acceptable levels of radioactivity which people could be exposed to. It was often multiplied from 10 to 50 times. The decision to continually alter the 'acceptable' levels was revealed in Russia's Constitutional Court when former second in command of the Politburo, Ligachev, told the Court that the artificial altering of the limits was for purely economic reasons. If the number of people who had to be evacuated could be kept down, roubles would be saved. As one cynical official said quietly to me, 'It is cheaper to bury them than to evacuate them. You know, if we evacuate, we must compensate and resettle them. Too many problems. It is better that they are left there.'

The suspiciousness and wariness I have found in the people affected by Chernobyl becomes fully understandable when you see how they have been so blatantly lied to and misled. In the aftermath of the accident, many herds of cattle had to be milked and then slaughtered but, instead of destroying the radioactive meat and milk, the authorities made yet another infamous Protocol. Protocol Number 32 reveals that 47,500 tons of radioactive meat was 'mixed' with clean meat and sold to the innocent, unsuspecting population of the USSR, along with 2 million gallons of radioactive milk. This appalling decision was taken to 'save' 1.7 million roubles. The meat and milk was consumed throughout the entire USSR, thus spreading the danger of radiation to far distant people and places.

The truth, yet again, has been the first casualty and has been hidden until now. We have finally managed to breach the wall of silence, deception and indifference. Ukrainian journalist Alla Yaroshinskaya, in speaking about the secret Protocols, claims that 'The most dangerous isotope to escape from the bleeding mouth of the reactor will never appear on the periodic chemistry scale. It is lie '86. A lie as global as the accident itself.' Her directness of truth-telling is an example to us all.

3

The truth finally starts to dawn

IN JANUARY 1991 Irish CND received a fax saying, 'SOS Appeal. For God's sake, help us to get the children out.' The fax was from Belarussian and American doctors who begged that the children be taken away from their radioactive environment so that some healing could be done. Our response was an immediate one, and our first group of Chernobyl children arrived in Ireland in the summer of 1991.

Since that time we have brought to Ireland over 1,000 children for rest and recuperation. Alongside the holiday visits, we started a medical aid programme which has 'adopted' 20 hospitals and orphanages in the contaminated regions of Belarus and western Russia.

The children have deeply touched us with their beauty, effervescence, love and friendship. It is one thing to know and understand what radioactivity does to a human being, but meeting, seeing and getting to know and love some of the victims of radiation is another story entirely.

In 1991 three women – Mary Aherne, Mary Murray and myself – became the first people from Ireland to visit the Chernobyl-affected area of Belarus. It was to be a harrowing experience. A lot of our time was spent in shock. I remember visiting a place where children had been abandoned by their parents, who were not able to cope with their babies' deformities or retardations. Seeing the pain of the babies and children suffering without the ease of pain-killers was practically unbearable. We saw babies with no brains, babies in permanent pain, with distorted and broken bodies. They were oblivious to life around them, locked inside their tormented shapes, awaiting death – a death which would end their short but pain-filled lives. We saw children without limbs, a little girl who

16

was so badly contorted that her legs grew up towards her body, youngsters with cruel mental handicaps and others with massive growths on their heads. The doctors and nurses, who loved their patients, could do little, since they lacked even the basic medicines.

Mothers and doctors alike made no secret of the fact that if they had had the equipment to identify the foetal defects in the womb, they would not have allowed these children to be brought into the world.

I held a little boy called Uri in my arms and literally felt his life draining away from him. A little boy, whose life was short and full of pain. His little face and his shrunken body will be one of the memories I will always carry with me. He died shortly after I took his photograph. The overwhelming memory I have of visiting this institution in Minsk is the sound of his crying, the doctors' crying and our own crying.

Men and women trained to protect and nurture life in both the institutions and the hospitals are at their wits' end and do not know what to do. They no longer have the medication, equipment or resources to sustain life. Dozens of babies await admission to this institution, which has only limited accommodation. Those who are accepted are the lucky ones, in the short term at least. It is just a 'holding place' for the children, and if they reach the age of four, they are committed to an adult mental asylum. We were unable to establish exactly which asylum they are sent to.

Many other children we met in a variety of institutions and state orphanages touched our hearts. I remember being in an orphanage close to the radiation zone and spending an afternoon with children who had been taken into state care because their parents were no longer capable of dealing with the scale of the tragedy in their lives. Little boys and girls, bursting to be loved and cuddled, danced and sang their hearts out in order to entertain these three Irish women who had come bringing toys, food and clothes. My breaking-point in one such orphanage came when a little girl tugged at the corner of my Irish cloak and slowly drew me to the door, crying 'Mama, Mama.' The look of expectation in that child's face was enough to break even the hardest heart.

Visiting the orphanages was always difficult. Conditions in most of them were similar. They were very cold, smelly and sparsely furnished. In one orphanage the children had to stay in their class-rooms from 8 a.m. until 10 p.m. because there was no place for them to go. During the holiday period there was very little to occupy their time. Most orphanages had food shortages and had practically no medicine. Many had no heating, despite the severity of the winters. Their main daily meal consisted of potatoes and macaroni.

What made it bearable was meeting the children who had been to Ireland for rest and recuperation. They were wonderfully enthusiastic and gave me lots of letters to take home to their 'Irish parents'. They often gathered around us and sang songs in Belarussian. They were always very sad to see us leave. The only consolation is that we continue to bring large groups of orphaned children abroad for holidays. The teachers and directors of the orphanages seemed to be good to the children, but such institu-tions are a very poor substitute for a family environment.

I remember speaking to Doctor Emma in one of the orphanages. She showed us the medicine cabinet containing only three small bottles of medicine, with no prospect of replacing even these, let alone obtaining any other supplies. There were two radioactive 'hot spots' near the orphanage and the doctors were fearful for the chil-dren and staff. Illness seems to be the order of the day. One of the medical workers, Ire, told us that her husband was ill in hospital and her daughter had cancer of the thyroid. She herself felt unwell but said she was 'afraid to die' because there was no one to look after her children. Her flat was miserable and depressing, just like her life. Her sorrow was etched in her face. Ire told us that many adults felt guilty and that somehow it was their fault that the accident happened.

Doctor Emma spoke about the accident. She remembered a strange smell, a metallic taste in the air. She didn't know what it was, but she kept the orphans indoors for a number of days as a precaution. She first heard of the accident on Freedom Radio (a US-funded radio station transmitting from Western Europe to the former USSR) and felt sure it was Western propaganda. But in case it was true, she gave a small dose of iodine to her family.

She claimed that the orphans' health had been affected by Chernobyl. Between 60–70% of the children had thyroid abnor-malities and weakened immune systems, causing many of the children to have liver, stomach and kidney problems. Dr Emma is a very kind woman, and as we parted she took off her watch and gave it to me as a gift.

Igor Pavolovetts was born on 30th March 1986 and became the first acknowledged 'deformed' victim as a direct result of Chernobyl. His mother, in despair and shock at the sight of his broken body, abandoned him at birth to the state authorities. He was four years old when we first met him and had never seen anything beyond the four walls of the institution. Igor was special from the first moment I met him, not only because of his physical difficulties but also because his bright and loving personality overcame his limited circumstances. Igor, along with 60 other children, was being kept in this 'holding place' which had little medicine, food or special facilities.

When I heard that he too would be committed to an adult mental asylum because he had survived beyond the age of four, I decided to take action. I subsequently brought the black-and-white stark photographs taken during that visit to the attention of retired businessman, Victor Mizzi, who spearheads The Chernobyl Children's Lifeline in England. This encounter was to change Igor's life forever. Victor's response to Igor's tragic plight was to fly to Minsk, and with our financial help he eventually succeeded in bringing Igor to England, where he was given a new arm and a new life. He has been made a ward of court and lives happily with a loving family in England.

Igor rarely talks about his life before being brought to England. The doctors maintain that because the experience was so traumatic, he is able to cope with the present only by burying the pain of his past. I had one of the most precious moments in my life when I was reunited with Igor in November 1994 at Victor Mizzi's home in Surrey. For this special reunion, I was accompanied by the key medic from the Irish Chernobyl Children's Project, Ann Norman.

I had only ever seen Igor at the institution in Minsk. The last time we had met was when we were filming the Irish documentary on Chernobyl. During that time, one by one, the crew had fallen in love with him. We returned on our last day in Belarus to play with Igor and the other children. He had got particularly attached to Liam, our producer, and Dónal, the cameraman, and darted

19

around the institution encouraging the two lads to pursue him and play. He was such a clever boy, and we knew that he knew that we had come from another world, a world different from his, a world that he felt he would never be a part of. His one and only hand clung around the neck of our producer as he gestured with the trunk of his tiny little body to ask us to take him with us. My last image of him was his sobbing, sad face, backed up against the wall, unable to look as we left.

All these memories came rushing back into my mind as I stepped into Victor's living-room and saw Igor sitting like a king on a bed of cushions, surrounded by Victor's dog, who was bigger than Igor! He stared intensely at me. I wondered if he would want to forget me, since I would be a painful association with the institution in Belarus. Getting down on my hands and knees, I kissed him gingerly. His direct stare and his grin gave me hope that he not only remembered me, but that the memories were happy ones. I took out some photos I had of him in 1991, along with some other boys and girls. Igor held them in his hand and fell quiet. I was afraid I had made a mistake and that he would withdraw from me into the memories the pictures evoked. But no! He laughed at himself and ran around the table to show them proudly to Barbara, his lovely foster mother.

I spent the next two precious hours crawling around the floor, with Igor shouting 'Catch me!' Because he was so tiny, he was able to run in and out under chairs and tables with great ease, and I felt a bit like Gulliver in the land of Lilliput, thumping around after him! He was so stunted that he only reached up to my knee. Every time I managed to catch him I gave him a kiss and told him I loved him. He'd look at me with his impish grin and lie on his back saying, 'Ticklish', which meant that I was to tickle him all over! He would immediately go into convulsions of laughter, which he knew would end up with another kiss from me!

During our prancing and playing, he pulled off his little socks and showed me his badly deformed feet. I was happy that he felt safe enough to expose his body's brokenness to me. Laughingly he gestured that he would cut off his strange feet, which are only pieces of muscle which twist around from back to front like little flippers. He grabbed a picture of a Belarussian teenager that he found in a pile of photos and told Ann and me that this was really him, 'Big Igor', and then said, 'I got squashed down tiny and my arm broke off, leaving me with just one arm.'

Every so often Ann and Victor had to try to draw my attention away from Igor to discuss our work on Chernobyl. Not much was done, as Igor and I kept distracting each other. When it came to leaving, Igor announced that he wanted to sit in the back 'with my girlfriend'! So we sat, hand in hand, and drove off to the railway station. As I waved goodbye, I felt an enormous pride in my heart. All the trials and tribulations attached to running the Project melted away! It was worth every ounce of energy just to see the happy face and hope-filled future of Igor.

4

Our twentieth-century Calvary

The ashes of Hiroshima are beating into our hearts
The ashes of Chernobyl are beating into our hearts
The ashes of all nuclear explosions that lie heavily on this earth
Are beating into our hearts.
Unknown Flemish Poet

In 1992, as the two Marys and I travelled deeper into the radiation zones, we were struck by the normality of people's lives. Farmers tilled their fields and herded their cattle, children played, mothers worked. The people affected by Chernobyl do not have the obvious signs of tragedy, such as the people in Bosnia or Ethiopia. The damage caused by radiation is invisible except in the eyes of the people, where you see despair and abandonment. Radiation is the silent, invisible enemy. It heeds no borders, travelling wherever the winds will carry it. It is an enemy that you cannot see, taste or touch, yet it is causing frightening damage to the whole cycle of life. There is a terrible foreboding of death and despair in the radiation zones. The social impact is unparalleled in human history. Whole communities of people have been separated through massive enforced evacuation. What has become of the ancient crafts, needlework, art and history of the villages that ended up inside the 30-kilometre exclusion zone? The ancient culture and heritage of Belarus stretches back a thousand years, with the roots of their race in the very area that has become known locally as 'death valley' and which can never be inhabited again due to radiation.

A Russian Orthodox priest whom we met in a little town in the zone told me once that Chernobyl is their 'twentieth-century Calvary'. This reference to the crucifixion is one that we witnessed not only in the words of the spiritual leaders, but also in the poetry and paintings of the people. A strong sense of persecution and death is rooted in the tragic history of Belarus. There are not many peoples to which history has been so cruel. More than once over the last 100 years it has seen its capacity for survival put to the test. For centuries their country, which has been the crossroads of Europe, has suffered invasion and aggression.

Wars and plagues have with terrible and implacable regularity at least once a century reduced the population by a quarter or a half. Between the middle of the seventeenth century and the end of the eighteenth, the population of the country was halved. At the end of the seventeenth century the population was reduced to fewer than one million people. The Belarussian race was on the brink of physical extinction. At the beginning of the nineteenth century they lost a quarter of the population. In the years of World War I a fifth of the population was lost, and during World War II one out of every four inhabitants was killed. Not one family remained untouched by the hand of death.

At the site of Khatyn, the local villagers were put to the torch along with the village by the Germans. In the Memorial Centre there are three birch trees to symbolize the survivors, and in place of the fourth tree burns an eternal flame. It took over 30 year for the population to reach its pre-war figure. Then came Chernobyl, the final straw for the Belarussian people. Their history has made them strong, but everyone has a threshold of pain beyond which the agony becomes too engulfing. The Belarussians are reaching that point.

The land in which we had arrived seemed like one of the starkest places on earth. The mourning and grieving we experienced in our first visit to Chernobyl is forever etched in my memory. On our return home I was unable to adjust for weeks. I had returned physically, but my heart and soul were left with the people of Belarus.

I became haunted by the sounds and images that my black-and-white photographs evoked. I fretted about the future of the children and their families. How could I tell the world about what had been cloaked in a shroud of secrecy and deception until now? Could I evoke a world response to the truth of this nuclear horror? With these questions came clarity of direction, and the seeds of what eventually became a world-class documentary began to gestate in my mind.

I had absolutely no background in film-making. If I had known then what I subsequently learned, the documentary would never have left my head! With an outline proposal for a documentary under my arm, off I went on the highways and byways of the Irish film world to see who was going to jump at the opportunity of both funding and making the documentary. Innocence is what carried me through! I was blessed that the first person I spoke to did not try to disillusion me but instead gave me encouragement and set me on the right road. I had chosen wisely in consulting Ireland's Minister for Arts, Culture and the Gaeltacht, Michael D. Higgins, and his wonderful wife Sabina. Around their kitchen table I spoke passionately about my dream of a film, and they set the ball rolling by putting me in touch with Irish film-makers.

Little by little I discovered that making a film is an expensive business and that I would need to raise a lot of money. CND was willing to put up all its money (£7,000), but it wouldn't be nearly enough for the production that I had in my head. Just when the whole idea was in a lull period, I got a phone call from Isobel Stephenson, who introduced herself as an independent film editor who had been given my proposal by the Columban Fathers while she was editing a programme for them. She was fascinated with the story and agreed to try and find a producer to talk to me. Things started to move quickly and within weeks I was discussing the making of the documentary with an independent Irish film production company.

The name of the company was DreamChaser and they were willing not only to make the documentary but also to pay for it! After initial negotiations, we approached a woman called Ali Hewson to join the team and be the presenter. Ali had no experience of film-making, but we felt that her charisma and dedication to the environment would bring a very special dimension to our programme. This decision was to prove to be an excellent one, and the gentle presence of Ali adds to the poignancy of the programme.

Rapid and intense meetings took place over a couple of weeks to discuss and decide what the thrust of the documentary would be. We all agreed that the film should be accessible to as wide an audience as possible.

In the middle of all the discussions about the programme's

outline and direction, the producer, Liam Cabot, was frantically organizing the equipment and crew, while I worked to confirm our itinerary in the Chernobyl regions of Belarus. Organizing anything in Belarus is a major hassle, and we had lots of moments when it seemed as if things were falling apart. On top of the technical and practical arrangements that needed to be made, I had to seek advice on how we could best protect ourselves against radiation while filming. Liam and I tried unsuccessfully to get radiation protection suits for ourselves. Everyone from the Department of Defence to Greenpeace refused us the precious suits because they would be useless afterwards. Strange logic! We eventually made do with chemical industry dust suits, complete with footwear and gloves. We bought the best possible masks we could find that would filter out radiation dust particles, thus completing what would become our protection against radiation.

Since food in the contaminated area would be risky, I also had to get a three-week supply of water and basic food – not an easy job considering that we would have weight and space restrictions on the aircraft and in our transport in Belarus. I ended up with three boxes of tuna fish in barbecue sauce, a box of sardines in oil, a box of butter, three boxes of Jacobs cream crackers, two boxes of Crack-a-wheat, a large tin of instant soup, two boxes of cheese, lots of chocolate and a large supply of toilet paper. Not a very exciting menu! After the food, my next problem was calculating the water supply we would need. When I looked at the volume laid out in front of me I visibly groaned! As it turned out, the water we brought was not sufficient and we had to spend the last three days without our own water supply.

On the morning of our departure (19th April 1993) we all met at Shannon Airport. This was the first time we had met one another. I remember feeling nervous, as we would have to spend three intense weeks together, and yet we were practically strangers. Ali, the quiet, studious one. Liam Cabot, the producer, always confident. Jerry Hoban, the director, forever 'Mr Cool'. Dónal Gilligan, the cameraman, and Dan Birch, the soundman, seemed like the wild ones. Isobel, the editor, was the calm one. During our flight out I remember Dónal and Dan asking me umpteen questions about Chernobyl. They had no notion of where they were about to find themselves and the possible danger involved. By the end of the flight they were a lot wiser. I bombarded them with so much information that they were contemplating getting the next plane home, only there wasn't a plane until the following week!

Ali studied scientific reports all the way to Minsk in between dipping into her cool box for vegetarian goodies. Ali was the healthy one. Isobel and Jerry slept. Liam studied his notes. Dónal, Dan and myself had a small 'getting to know you' Irish whiskey (or two!). The most exciting part of the journey was when Jerry woke up, looked out of his window and saw the engine on fire. Luckily enough, we were about to land, and we were all saved. So their 'baptism' into Belarus was really one of fire.

Reeling from the fright of the engine, we landed at Minsk airport to be faced with our first experience of the 'new' Belarus. It came in the guise of a $60 entrance fee into the country! We were taken aback and argued that the fee should be waived. The heated discussion was between ourselves and three guards, neither of us understanding each other's language, but nonetheless understanding each other's body language! We pleaded that since we were there to make a documentary which would tell the world the tragedy of Belarus, surely we deserved to have the entry fee defrayed. Eventually, after much tutting, they let us enter the country for nothing.

We spent the next couple of days listening to the usual official 'It's not possible', or 'It's a problem', in response to what we needed to do in order to make the documentary. It seemed as if we would be unable to film in the deserted villages or in the 'purple zone' (the colour purple is used on the radiation maps to show the most heavily contaminated areas). But the Belarussians soon learned that our politeness was not weakness, and eventually we succeeded in getting on the road to Chernobyl to make our film.

5

Blotting out the radiation

THE FIRST PLACE we visited was a special institution known locally as 'the liquidator's place', officially called the Centre for Radiation Research. In its former Soviet life, it was a luxury retreat for the *crème de la crème* of the Communist Party. They chose their hiding place well: set among the forests, in front of a lake, far from the eyes of the people. Now it serves as the medical and monitoring centre for people throughout Belarus who have been affected by Chernobyl.

It is home also to a very special group of men called 'liquidators' or 'bio-robots'. We spoke to these men to hear exactly what their work had been at the reactor and to find out why they had been given these strange names.

The first man we spoke to had been in charge of the robots which had been brought in from Germany and Japan to remove the highly radioactive graphite from the reactor's core. The robots ceased to function because the levels of radiation were too high. That was when they conscripted in 600,000 human 'bio-robots' for the clean-up. The conscripted men were farmers, miners and factory workers from throughout the USSR. They became the 'liquidators'. They unwittingly exposed themselves to massive doses of radiation. According to the survivors, the decision to use humans had not been based on scientific or technical grounds but on political ones. The job was to be done at any cost as quickly as possible. Many scientists objected strongly, but they were not listened to. The 'liquidators' were deemed heroes in 1986 but are now discarded and forgotten, vainly trying to establish that their ill health is the result of the extraordinary levels of radiation to which they were exposed.

The conscripts received insufficient protective clothing to carry out their work; in some cases none at all. Sometimes the men had to lift pieces of radioactive graphite with their bare hands. They had to fight the 300 fires which had been created as chunks of the reactor had been scattered all over the Chernobyl site. They had to dig holes under the convulsing reactor, shovel hot waste off the adjoining roof, and strip contaminated land. Much of this work was done with minimum protection. The men told us how officials had ignored radiation levels during the clean-up and had even deliberately obstructed efforts by some to monitor the doses that the workers were receiving.

One of the younger 'liquidators' told us that his wife had given birth to a baby the week before his conscription. Ashen-faced with anger, he told us that the job he had been given to do had exposed him to extremely high radiation levels. He was part of a team decontaminating a village. He was exposed not only to radiation, but also to the mysterious chemical 'cocktails' that had been used in the decontamination process. The village they worked in was recontaminated the following week. They had risked their health and their future for nothing. This young man fears that he will not live to see his baby grow up.

The men spoke not only about their personal fears for themselves and their families, but also about the lack of action concerning the millions of acres of heavily contaminated land and the hundreds of uncategorized radioactive waste disposal sites scattered throughout the zone. There are 77 authorized nuclear waste dumps in Belarus alone, and because the dumps were being filled in a hurry in the midst of a chaotic and panic-stricken crisis, many of the sites do not meet the required safety standards. Little is known about the quantity and radiochemical composition of the waste placed into these dumps. Clothing, toys and cars were tipped into these huge clay-lined trench dumps. They told us that when the dumps were full, they had to line up and leave row upon row of contaminated trucks, fire engines and military vehicles awaiting a decision about what to do with them. The men did their best, but there were very few people with scientific expertise to advise them about the dumps. So the people of Belarus are faced with yet another tentacle of the Chernobyl monster.

A man called Igor Shik, a former laundry worker, had been

conscripted to the Bragin region. Igor stayed for the minimum conscription time of 180 days, from 1st June to 24th October 1986. Many of his friends stayed for one year, since they had no jobs to return to. Igor and his team worked on evacuating families, removing radioactive topsoil, and cutting down radioactive forests. Around Chernobyl entire forests were felled, and the concept of 'Red Forest' was born. They left one fir tree standing as a special memorial to 200 Russian partisans who had been hanged there by the Germans during the war.

Igor told us that once the job of decontamination was done in a village, a special monitoring vehicle would drive through it to test the radiation levels. The men knew that their work had been successful if the two flags on the vehicle stood up straight. If the flags fell down, it meant that the levels were still high. Follow-up checks would be made just days later, and the men would be dismayed to see that the flags that had been upright had dropped miserably, indicating that the area had been recontaminated. All their work, putting their lives at risk, had been for nothing. In the meantime the evacuated families had returned to what was still a radioactive village. When asked about the material used in the decontamination of the houses, Igor said that it appeared to be ordinary washing powder.

He told us that they were given practically no protective clothing. What minimum protective gear they had was too hot to work in and was soon discarded. The masks they used stuck to their faces and caused rashes, so the men took them off.

They were promised weekly doctor's check-ups. None happened. When their blood was finally tested, it registered very high radiation. The testing ceased in order to stop the men from panicking. At no stage were they given iodine (which would have protected their thyroid glands) in either liquid or tablet form. Nor did they have access to a geiger counter to measure the doses of radiation to which they were being exposed.

For months on end the 'liquidators' slept in tents. Each night the tents were sprayed with some mysterious powder which was supposed to reduce the radiation levels. To prevent the radiation affecting their health, they were given extra food: one egg, milk, fruit juice and butter. As 'compensation', Igor and his friends were given an extra two weeks' holiday a year and free local transport in Minsk.

Igor has no home and currently lives in very cramped conditions in his parents' flat. For Igor to buy a flat would cost him $20,000. Since he has to live on $5 a month, there is little prospect that he and his family will ever have their own home. His wife has been seriously ill in hospital for the past year and he believes that he is responsible for her illness. His son, born since the accident, is also seriously ill.

When we asked him why he stayed in the radiation zone, he told us that all the men were warned that their families would be severely punished if they did not serve their minimum time.

Another man, Vitaly, spoke in rushed words about how full of excitement the men had been as they gathered at the train station in late May 1986 before they departed to do some 'secret' work. He said the mood among the conscripts was 'one of fun, like boys going to pioneer camp. There were some 7,000 of us reservists on this specially chartered train. Officially we were called "tourists". It seems like a sick joke now.

'We lived in tents and the only thing that kept us going was the promise that once the Chernobyl block was cleaned up we would all be sent home. We were all very happy when, after two weeks of demolishing villages, we were finally called to start work on the five roofs over Reactor 3.

'The roofs had been given names by the men who had worked before us, all women's names: Lyena, Marsha, Katya, Natasha and Anna. Oh, Marsha was the mad one. She was right over the exploded area and was cut open like a wound. We had to cross over several wooden gangplanks from one roof to the next and the faster you ran, the less radiation you got! All we had to wear against this stuff was our cotton uniform, a lead apron, lead pants and a cotton helmet which had a glass visor.

'This was an insane time in all of our lives. God, to think about it makes me cry. We were living on the edge of our lives all the time. Imagine, we had only 60 and sometimes only 5 seconds to do our work on the roof! Any more time there, and we were exposing ourselves to lethal doses of the stuff. To cut out any chance of taking too much time, we used to do a practice run on the ground to help us speed up. When we worked on the roof, we were under camera surveillance, and the idea was that if one man collapsed it would be seen and a siren would sound, and the man's partner would drag him away.

'You know something? It's funny, but the reality was not always the same as the theory. I tell you this and swear it's the truth. We couldn't wear the lead pants. They were impossible to wear because they cut into our legs and we couldn't run, so most of us didn't wear them. We stopped laughing very soon after we arrived in this hell place. Many of us from the group started to have great difficulties breathing, so the running got harder. We began to be dizzy and to vomit, and balancing on the planks became harder and harder. Some of the men were taken away and we heard rumours that they had gone to Moscow for treatment. I don't know the truth. We never saw those men again.'

There was a quiet, shy man, perhaps in his late twenties, who eventually spoke. His name was Ruslan and he told us how he and his friends had been used as human geiger counters. They had been sent into fields that were so radioactive that none of the counters could register the levels. This was how they made the radiation maps: any area where the levels went off the scale became known officially as the most radioactive areas, and on the maps these were denoted by the colour purple. After their job was completed these men were told to take off their clothes and to have a good scrub in the shower. Afterwards they were 'rewarded' with lots of vodka and a special card calling them 'good patriots'.

Sitting beside Ruslan was a large man with very weather-beaten features. His name was Vadim. 'I have changes in my blood, less energy, and sometimes my liver is very bad,' he said. 'I was sent to Moscow because of the pains, especially the ones in my stomach and the bones of my feet. A small piece of radioactive fuel stuck to my pants and I didn't know it for a couple of days, and when I got measured, my right leg had a dose of 5,000 rems. I'm just waiting to die now. It will happen. Like the others. Maybe when I sit in the chair or just lie in my bed.'

The men sat before us in a row, young men awaiting death, smiling briefly while I took some photographs. Each of them held up their special 'liquidator' identification card declaring them to be national heroes. There is a terrible sense of abandonment, isolation and despair among these men.

During the course of our interview with five of these men, we listened and empathized with the experiences they shared. The air was fraught with anger and tension from the men. The film crew sat immobilized by the insanity of the story. Only their pure professionalism ensured that their emotions did not overwhelm the necessity to film and record the story of how these young men had been lied to and abused by their government, and now were left to their own devices to survive. The 'liquidators' have formed a survivors' organization. The membership keeps decreasing, not from lack of interest on the part of the members, but because they are dying. To date, approximately 13,000 of these special men have died. Almost 20% of these deaths were suicides. This is 20 times higher than the international average. A further 70,000 are estimated to be permanently disabled.

Because they were conscripted from throughout the USSR, it is impossible to keep a medical check on the majority of the men. Most of them will never have their health monitored. The authorities, it seems, have deliberately not even kept records or have just 'lost' radiation data which would give vital information on how much radiation the men absorbed. Many of them received more than ten times the recommended doses in a couple of minutes. In just 90 seconds, the men received the maximum lifetime dose.

We spoke to one of the doctors, who also called himself a 'liquidator' because he worked with the men in the reactor. He told us how he had seen the authorities tamper with the geiger counter readings to ensure that the levels appeared reasonable. He said that these altered levels became known among the workers as 'administrative doses'. This act of callousness cost the lives of thousands of men and has rendered thousands more the 'living dead'. These men and their families are under enormous mental pressure. They have little left to live for. All they were given was a certificate declaring their heroism, and they carry a special card defining them as 'liquidators', which gives them some small privileges.

In the Soviet Union's view, the fight against the consequences of radiation took on heroic proportions. Terms such as 'blotting out the radiation', calling fire fighters 'heroes' and the clean-up workers 'liquidators' are just examples of how the authorities tried to portray the accident and the radiation as enemies needing to be defeated. There is little to be triumphant about.

The 'liquidators' described bulldozing hundreds of towns and villages into the ground. Places that had existed for a thousand years were wiped off the map. Hundreds of other villages were submerged in concrete or burned to the ground. More than 4 million cubic metres of earth were dug up and stored in 800 shallow graves around the radiation zone. The earth around the streets and gardens of the towns and villages was dug up to the depth of 20 centimetres. The 'liquidators' also had to carry out the awful task of forcing hundreds of thousands of terrified peasant people onto buses during the evacuations.

These 'disposable' men will never be the same; neither will their families. It is thanks to the bravery of Validimir Chernousenko, the chief scientist in the 'exclusion zone', that the story of the 'liquidators' ever reached the foreign press. Formerly he worked at Kiev's Academy of Sciences, and he received lethal doses of radiation in his frantic effort to clear up the radioactive debris that littered the reactor site. The doctors estimate that he has five years left to live. He lost his job at the Academy for telling the truth and had to flee to Germany, assisted by Euro MP Petra Kelly. Chernousenko was the executive adviser as well as the co-author of the official report on Chernobyl commissioned by President Gorbachev.

Some of the concerned scientists took their story and evidence to an international congress at Vienna in August 1986. Valery Legasov, the head of the Soviet delegation, gave extensive information about the true scale of the accident and why he believed it had happened. His words were largely ignored by those present. In the memoirs he left behind he expresses his anger and despair about the safety of nuclear energy in the Soviet Union. He wrote that he had wanted to study the safety problems of the particular Chernobyl reactor, and for this very reason was opposed by those who said there were no problems with the Chernobyl-type reactors. Legasov finally talks about a 'certain inevitability' of an accident at Chernobyl.

He said, 'The scope of the efforts which have become necessary for the elimination of the consequences of this nuclear accident shows that mankind will not be able to survive a nuclear war.' He continued, 'Today no task is more pressing and noble, not only for a scientist, but also for any sober-minded individual, than to prevent nuclear insanity.' In 1988 Legasov, no longer able to cope with the consequences of the accident, committed suicide.

6

The misplaced and displaced ones

I N THE DAYS and weeks after the accident a major evacuation plan was implemented. For many people the first they heard of the accident was when army tanks and buses came through their streets and men dressed in strange white costumes shouted out through loud-hailers, telling the people to get out of their beds and leave their houses forever. In the terrifying confusion that followed, many families were separated and sent to different evacuation centres. It often took families weeks to find each other.

The authorities confiscated dosimeters (for registering radiation levels) from all individuals and institutes in the area in order to keep the radiation levels and consequences a secret. Not only that, but the Politbureau signed a secret protocol authorizing the altering of the so-called 'acceptable' levels of radiation, sometimes by a factor of 50. I find myself so angry when people talk about how much radiation we can take. What we should be saying is that all levels of radiation are 'unacceptable', and we should work towards eliminating all man-made sources. Adding to the unavoidable dose received from natural radiation sources possibly will be one of humankind's greatest follies and regrets.

Over 400,000 people have already been relocated. They have become environmental refugees. The area they left is now a radiation desert composed of depopulated no-go areas covering many thousands of hectares, fenced off with barbed wire. It is a haunting monument to humanity's destructive capability. Evacuations will continue long into the next century because new areas of contamination are found every day.

Those who remain in the zones have to change their lifestyle drastically. They are supposed to change their clothes twice a day, for instance. They may not walk for more than two hours a month in the contaminated woods. They may not grow their own food.

Imagine the life of every living individual in the zone, who must organize his or her life around the radiation level charts printed daily in local newspapers. They live under the sword of Damocles. A mere glance at these charts will make it clear how complex and unprecedented the situation is. One in four of the population of Belarus has become an innocent victim of Chernobyl, of an atomic Armageddon, hostages to the hazardous aftermath of radiation. When the first radiation maps appeared in national newspapers, it immediately became apparent that the contamination was much more extensive than had previously been believed. It is currently estimated that over 40% of Belarus was affected.

Even during the days and months immediately after the accident, in thousands of villages and towns stretching for hundreds of kilometres away from the reactor, people continued to harvest their crops, drink their milk, feed their livestock and eat their home-grown vegetables. There were no restrictions imposed on the consumption of milk or the milking of cows, and no one received iodine tablets. In fact, for the following four years people produced and ate from their contaminated soil. People living in clean areas also had to consume contaminated produce, since there was no other access to food.

While travelling to Gomel on our first day in the radiation zone, we stopped to talk to some farmers to hear if Chernobyl had changed their lives in any way. We were unprepared for the stories that we were told. As we stopped at the side of the road, more and more people came out from the fields and communicated one bizarre story after another.

It was mainly the women who spoke. They cried bitter tears of anger and frustration at how their lives were locked into the effects of Chernobyl. Farmers are instructed to observe ludicrous rules, such as limiting the amount of time spent outdoors, keeping doors and windows closed, and leaving wellington boots and farming shoes outside the door. There are rules for indoors as well, such as implementing a much stronger regime of cleanliness, washing living rooms more often, leaving work clothes outside, spraying ashes with water before cleaning the fireplace, and drying dishes, crockery and cutlery thoroughly in order to limit the doses of radiation. People in the zones are encouraged to have a more nutritious high-protein diet which is supposed to improve resistance against internal radiation and to lower absorption of cesium 137 and strontium 90.

One woman spoke angrily about the 'death money' they are given by the authorities which is supposed to be used to buy uncontaminated food. She pointed out that since most shops, particularly in the villages, are empty, people are forced to eat their own contaminated food.

Farmers are given itemized lists of vegetables, the most radioactive ones on the top of the list and graduating downward. One of the farmers translated the list and gave it to us as follows: cabbage, cucumbers, tomatoes, onions, garlic, potatoes, carrots, beetroot, radishes, peas, beans and sorrel. He told us that red- and black-currants were the most dangerous fruits and to a lesser degree cultivated strawberries, apples and pears.

Farmers are warned about organic farming practices that can increase the levels of radionuclides. For example, they are supposed to check their fire ashes for radiation before using them on their compost heaps. They are advised that, after harvest, old leaves and other vegetation that would normally be composted should be destroyed.

Housewives in the zones told of even more bizarre instructions for the preparation of food. Vegetables and fruit were supposed to be washed in 'clean water' – of course, no one is told where this clean water is to be found. The removal of skins, the external leaves of cabbages and the heads of root vegetables, they are told, will also reduce the radioactivity. All fruit and vegetables are to be washed at least five times.

Regarding the keeping and feeding of livestock, the farmers told us that for hay and pastures they had to try to select the least contaminated areas. Cattle should not be let out to graze when grass was less than ten centimetres high, so that they would not touch the earth. It was recommended that cows and goats should be fed in their stalls and only by foodstuffs from the least contaminated areas.

Preparing milk for family consumption was another crazy story. The farmers were told that, to reduce the radioactive contamination, the cream had to be separated and the fatless milk used for making cheese. The remaining liquid should not be used, and there were no instructions about how to dispose of it. Because radionuclides remain in buttermilk, the farmers were told that they must use an elaborate filtering system to try and clean out the radioactivity.

People were told that if they pickled their meat the radiation would be reduced. They were also supposed to wash the meat constantly with clean water. Once more, no one had any idea where to get the water or what to do with it once it had been used.

These old men and women had few choices in their lives. As one woman said, 'If we don't eat the radioactive food, we will starve.'

Approximately 2,000 towns and villages have been evacuated. These depopulated areas will be uninhabitable for hundreds of years, even according to the most optimistic estimates. At least another 70,000 people in Belarus are still awaiting evacuation. But to where? Many of the evacuees that we spoke to have ended up being uprooted for nothing. They discovered that the areas where they were moved to became as contaminated as the places they had left. The situation is complicated. In one village we discovered that the houses were fit to live in, but the fields around the village could not be used for growing food. In the next village the opposite was the case.

Farm workers from a collective farm situated not far from the radioactive area said their children complained about always being sick. They ate contaminated food and they drank contaminated milk. One mother said, 'Who cares about our children? No one.' Standing, staring, listening to her mother talk, a child of about ten responded to my question about her health by saying, 'It's just the sickness of the children. That's all.' The farm where they live produces 8,000 litres of milk from 900 cows every day. Milk production continued during and after the accident. Despite the officially permitted levels being altered many times since 1986, the farmers have been told that their milk is within acceptable limits.

The woman said, 'We wanted to be evacuated. We've waited all this time. Why are we being left here? To die, is it? Why have they not fenced off this land like over there? Everyone comes with their machines. We hear the bleep-bleep-bleep and then those men go away and don't come back to help us. We all want to go.'

This woman's story is unfortunately just another sad example of the crisis of a poisoned land and a broken people. Professor Vasily

Nesterenko (one of the surviving scientists who participated in the damage assessment flights over the burned-out reactor) has commented, 'During World War II 280 of our villages were burnt to the ground by the Nazis, but now 3,000 villages are burning slowly from radiation poison. They should be evacuated, but our Government refuse. Our death is slowly emerging.'

With the benefit of hindsight, we can now state that when the evacuations from the exclusion zone finally took place they were grossly inadequate and, for many, came too late. They were lengthly and disorderly and took twelve long weeks, until June 1986, to complete. From then on, there was a bizarre belief that the fence surrounding the exclusion zones would somehow control the movement of radiation.

We visited two evacuee towns outside Minsk. In Shabani over 10,000 people lived in a concrete jungle of 15-storey, character-less, functional buildings. Malinovka was no different. It housed 11,000 evacuees, of whom 5,000 were children. Most of the people were peasant farmers who were now landless and jobless. Who wants the skills of a farmer (who may be illiterate) in a big, sprawling city? The stress and strain caused by the evacuations has resulted in huge social unrest. Six out of every ten marriages now end in divorce. Many of the people we spoke to said that their living standards had worsened and that a lot of added stress had been created by the break with their cultural and historical values which had been caused by the forced removal from their lands.

In both evacuee centres we heard how the people, referred to as 'the Chernobyls', are often hated and isolated. This stigma has deeply hurt and offended them, and causes terrible division within their new settlements.

The stories shared with us were difficult to hear. A young woman told us that at the time of the evacuations she was pregnant. She subsequently gave birth to a little girl called Lydia, who was born with stunted growth, immune system problems and a severe thyroid difficulty. The mother had been made sterile by the radiation doses she received. The father was now unemployed and tried his best to eke out a living as a labourer.

According to the director of the evacuee organization in Malinovka, 95% of the children are ill. They are tested only every six months and very little information is given about the results.

Seven women evacuees came and told us their stories. Tanya told us how she had to bring her furniture with her, even though she knew it was contaminated, but she had no option because she had no money to buy new furniture for her otherwise bare flat.

Tamara spoke about the 'black sticky rain' that fell after the accident. It ran down her face and stained her clothes. She also revealed that when the local villagers pleaded with the authorities to evacuate the children and pregnant women, they were rebuffed. The authorities chose to evacuate 100,000 cattle in preference to the women and children. Tamara spoke about the 'bandits' who hid in the evacuated villages. She had spoken to some of them, who had come all the way from Moldavia. They had said, 'It's better to die slowly from radiation than to die from a bullet in the war.' (They were referring to the on-going war between the newly independent state of Moldava and its break-way ethnic Russian region of Dnestva.) Tamara wanted to take her family to a clean area for a short while after the accident, but she was told she would be dismissed from her job if she 'dared' to leave. She needed the income from her job, so she and her family stayed.

Tatyana told us how she was compelled to feed her family radioactive food. She had no other choice. Her husband had died the year before, aged 36. She was convinced it was because of Chernobyl. She and her family had lived in the zone for six years, awaiting evacuation.

Natasha cried as she told us how her husband had left her and their two children, aged five and seven, because he couldn't take the added pressure in their lives. Her son is extremely ill and Natasha has to carry him. Her added agony is that the authorities will not recognize her son as a 'Chernobyl invalid'. They were not evacuated until 1993.

Gallina and her family have to share a tiny apartment with another family. She receives $5 a month on which to survive. She never knew anything about the accident. Her children remained outdoors during the crucial days while the reactor burned. After her village had been 'decontaminated', her son had become very ill and had never recovered. He now had a severe liver problem, but was given no medicine for it.

Marsha's son, who was born in April 1986, never left hospital for the first three years of his life. He appeared perfect at birth but almost immediately fell ill. Now he could not speak, and he had heart problems. Marsha's husband was a 'liquidator'.

Anna talked about her daughter Tanya, who was also born in April 1986. Tanya was now severely affected by a variety of health problems. When she had been tested as a baby, the dosimeter had gone off the scale. Anna had twelve other children, all of whom had been diagnosed with thyroid abnormalities. One of her children had had her thyroid removed.

All seven women and their families were representative of the evacuees. Many of them were very poorly dressed and unable to work because they had to take care of their sick children. Each of their children had a special government certificate declaring them 'Chernobyl invalids'. This stigmatized them as victims, and was a permanent reminder of their plight. None were fit enough to go to school. They all wet their beds at night. Thanks to the courage of these women, a small community organization had been formed to try to get help for the evacuees. We found very few such community groups in our travels. We would like to see a lot more, because it is important that people should start to empower themselves. Most people were afraid to organize for fear of repercussions. The isolation and stress in the lives of these innocent women were unbearable.

We met with the Satsura family. Originally from a place called Khoniki, they had been evacuated in 1992. Mrs Satsura sat and talked with us with her daughter Natasha on her lap and her son Igor by her side. Mrs Satsura told us that Igor had cancer of the thyroid gland and Natasha had a severe liver complaint and would only live for another five years at the most. Mrs Satsura also had a thyroid problem. 'I would give anything for the health of my children,' she said. Her children silently listened as their mother told of her fears. Natasha, white as a sheet, squeezed her mother's hand in silent anxiety. Igor watched and stared. The clock on the wall ticked. It was the only thing that seemed normal in the abnormality of their lives.

The children's ailing granny sat and stared directly into our eyes and raised her hands in despair, clutching her head, moving her body forward and backward. We didn't know her language but we understood her pain.

As we left, Mrs Satsura insisted on our taking three jars of preserved fruit as a gift. She told us proudly how she had managed to save the last of the berries from her old garden in Khoniki, and she wanted to offer them to us in gratitude for hearing her story. We politely took the jars and offered thanks, but we knew that the gift must be dumped because the berries would more than likely be contaminated.

We spoke to Nicolai Dorogatzev, a vet, who had lived for five years in the radiation zone. He told us about the animal deformities that he saw in the zone: animals born with five legs or two heads or four eyes. Within just months of the accident he delivered animals born with no skin; others were not even recognizable, but were just lumps of jelly-like flesh. His daughter Marsha suffered from the radiation. His wife was in hospital and there was no treatment for her.

One old woman refugee we visited showed us how, for the old people especially, the evacuations were the beginning of the end. Terrified of the city she was now forced to live in, with no way of sustaining herself financially, she was totally dependent on the charity of her neighbours and on the 'coffin money' of 30 roubles a month. This was the first time I had heard of the terrible words 'coffin money', a term used for the miserable contribution given by the state to evacuees. She had no shoes, just paper on her feet. This woman told us, with great sadness, of how she had once had a house, a pig, some chickens, and land to grow vegetables. For the land that had supported her family for generations, and for all of her worldly possessions, she was given the sum of $5. This old woman told us she had nothing left to live for.

The same stories cropped up in every evacuee centre we visited. In an evacuee village outside the city of Gorky we were shocked by the living conditions. Houses of very poor quality, built in a hurry with the cheapest of materials, were inadequate substitutes for the lovely 200-year-old cottages the evacuees had left behind. When we visited this village in five feet of snow, the houses reeked of dampness and had little or no heating. Some of the people had no electricity, no medicine and little food. Children, lurking behind the doors, had scant clothing and no footwear. These families were trying to survive on $6 a month. One family had lost two babies and their third was seriously ill.

Another woman cried as she held her ill child in her arms and told us we could not take a photograph of her or her child. Too many foreign delegations had come and she had shed her tears, opened her heart and told of her pain in the hope that help would come, but nothing ever came. This shy woman said neither she nor her family and friends were a 'human zoo' to be looked at, probed at, or photographed. What little dignity she had left she wanted to keep private.

In the same evacuee village we sat and talked with the people about what they remembered about April 1986, and this was where we heard again about the 'black sticky rain' that came down in the early warm days of May. This 'black rain' was very unusual and marked people's clothing and skin and took a long time to wear off. Enquiring about this strange rain, we were later told that it had been caused by the effects of the 'cloud seeding' that had been ordered by Moscow. Apparently several military aircraft were ordered to spray the radioactive cloud which hung over parts of Belarus and Russia in order to force a change in the weather. This calculation decided who would be contaminated and who would not. We live in strange times when we give governments powers of life and death over innocent people.

The evacuations have by no means solved the problems. Now Belarussian evacuees who were sent to live in the Baltic states after the accident are being thrown out by the new governments because they are seen as an unnecessary economic burden. They have no alternative but to return to Belarus. Since there is nowhere to go, they return secretly to the deserted villages and hide out. These people have nowhere else to go and they live in fear of the special, fully armed police units finding them. The police told us about them when we were filming. They warned us that these people 'might be dangerous'.

The threat to the 'hidden ones' is very real. One time we were secretly being taken around a deserted village in the Gomel region, and we came upon an old man and his sister. They had been evacuated initially in 1987 but had subsequently returned because they were unable to identify with their strange new urban life. They had been caught many times by the police and each time had been forcibly removed, only to return again and again to their house. The old family home was cold, dark and squalid, but nonetheless home.

For the evacuees in the cities there are a host of difficulties to be faced. Unemployment is a major problem, since there is little or no demand for their farming skills in the cities. With no prospects for their future, new social problems emerge. The old people are undergoing major adjustment difficulties because they find it soul-destroying to try to live in a city. They are returning in ever-increasing numbers to live in the world's most radioactive environment. When we shared their cramped living conditions in these high-rise city buildings we understood their unhappiness.

A further sad footnote to this story is that UNESCO reports that poor people from throughout the three affected countries are moving back into the contaminated regions in order to receive special state benefits.

7

Victims' witness

THE POWER AND strength of the survivors' stories and poetry have left a marked impression on me. Children who speak about a new way of counting time: 'before and after Chernobyl'. Children whose memories are divided and scarred into 'life and death': 'life' was before, 'death' is now. Their testimonies are a powerful witness to human suffering and act as a forewarning of what might befall all of us unless we take heed.

Chernobyl

(Written by children from the radiation zone with the assistance of their teacher, Gallina Temchina.)

Look! The children from Belarus are crippled
Why such grief? Why such deceit?
Tell us please who is to answer?
Tell us!
Now the time has come
One should answer for what is done
Remember!
Stop!
Reflect in anger!
The children of this world want to live
Stand up please!
I implore you, people,
Stand up hand in hand
Be kind, giving.
Look at your children and weep
Cry, and appeal
Strike the bell.

We are the children of Chernobyl,
We want to live, to laugh, to grow, to love
But we are doomed.
We have no future.
We plead with you mothers and fathers
Help us.
Help us.
Will you hear?
Unite to work for a better cause
You are people and you are not of stone.
Help us. Please?

Svetlana's story

'When we start speaking about the disaster we should begin by speaking about our lives. We now consider our lives before and after Chernobyl, and I remember perfectly well the time when it came to us. I happened all in one night, but nobody knew it. It was very dangerous because the weather was unusually hot during those days. Usually in April the weather is rather cool or cold and during those days it was very hot. All the people were very glad to be outside and to get a little bit of sunshine.

'It was Saturday and Sunday and people were in the streets, but something had happened because in the evening of the next day my brother telephoned me and he told me something very strange. I didn't understand him very well. He was supervising some military department, a kind of service there in our atomic facility. He told me to keep inside and not to go out. He said something was strange, because inside the institute it was quite okay. The dosimeters didn't show anything. But outside the dosimeters fell behind the scales. It was strange, they could not understand what was going on.

'Later on, some hours later, they tried to get in contact with the special committees for our civil protection. They could not give a direct answer because they were not allowed. They didn't know themselves, and only some days later we got to know what happened. Certainly it was too late, because our thyroids had already absorbed all the radioactive elements. Our thyroids were ruined.

'On 1st May we had our usual May Day parades and all our people were brought to them all over the country. They were not cancelled, it was very strange. People knew a little about the accident but, you know, when danger is not seen, it is not felt. It was very unreal for people to understand that they had already been contaminated. When I met my pupil in the street, she was walking with her baby in the pram. I told her, "Go away, stay at home." She said, "Why should I? What's the problem? The weather is so nice." They could not understand, they didn't believe; it was like a silent death. I remember I was shocked when we walked past our Parade stand, with all the leaders and the army, to see they were dressed in white radiation suits! We were there with bare arms and legs! What was the matter?

'I am a teacher and I was asked to volunteer to take care of these children called "Chernobyl Children". They were the first to be brought to a special place outside Minsk. I had a chance, a tragic one, to work with very little children. They were five, six, seven years of age only and they stayed for two months in Minsk Hospital. They were very ill. They were deprived of their mothers for the first time. They were all country peasant children. Some of them were very self-restrained: they were very shy. They couldn't get accustomed to this new environment. Those children were taken away from their homes all of a sudden and now they were very ill. They were frightened and confused.

'It was the first time I felt the reality. The most tragic thing was when the children were arriving in dozens of buses, we were put in some special suits for protection from the children. That was such a dreadful sight. I took off my suit to comfort the children. My job was to decontaminate them. I had to take off all their clothes and wash down the children. We didn't know what to do with those clothes. They were very contaminated. All their clothes were taken away. But then we had the problem of where to take those clothes. They could not be burnt, because all the radiation would go up. So we decided to bury them. Again, where to bury them?

'But the most tragic thing was that the children themselves were radioactive. They radiated to such a degree that when we were checked later on, I myself started to radiate – my liver, my thyroid and especially my feet. Their clothes gave off such a great radiation that I was afraid. When I looked at the dosimeter it began to move before my eyes and make a noise – d-d-d-d-d-d – oh, it was really startling. I was scared very much indeed myself.

'We applied to our factories and authorities to help us because those children came from the most contaminated zone and we wanted to have them taken somewhere else which was safe. We received little help. They were practically vanishing before our eyes. They were becoming pale, even blue in their faces. Their blood pressure was terrible, they were vomiting all the time. My little ones could not stay in bed because they were crying for their mothers all the time. They struggled with me, sometimes they threw my glasses off. Something terrible was happening to all our children. They could not eat. The state budget was so very poor, and we got no help.

'It was like a nightmare. Can you imagine? Some children were given special identity labels – red, green or yellow. If a child got a red label nobody could approach him or touch him. If he had a green label, that was bad but not so terrible. Yellow was okay.

'Another thing – we teachers that volunteered had to bring our own children, since we had no one to mind them. We tried to keep them aside somehow; we put them in a special building and they were separated, but still they are children, you know, and we could not separate them for ever. They played together, and that's why our children got some portion of the radiation. That was the most terrible thing. I have only my one son, you see.

'These children were blocked on one of the floors – they were not allowed to go anywhere. That depressed them so much. Can you imagine? When parents came to visit their children they were not allowed to see them! They didn't know what to do. Some of them were so desperate that they took their own lives, believing they would never see their children again. This lasted for 60 days.

'I will never forget the mornings. It was terrible. We had to line them up in the square, and it was to become the routine of our camp life. One by one the children fell. They could not stand even for five minutes. They fell down and we took them away in pairs sometimes. It was a dreadful sight. I then began to realize that something so awful had happened.'

Emma's story

'It's not so easy for a mother and granny to share sad experiences, especially if they concern children. The emotional damage to our people is a terrible thing.

'Two weeks after the accident I was returning home by train from visiting my son in Moscow, who was serving time in the army. There were four of us in the compartment. I have very vague memories of two men who were in the same compartment with me, the but face of the third stands out quite vividly in my memory. He was a soldier, a boy of 19. He was overwhelmed with sorrow; there was no joy in his eyes. He couldn't forget the last couple of days of his life. He was one of those participating in burying the perished from Chernobyl. Here is his story.

'"Five dead firemen were brought to the cemetery in Moscow. There were five groups of soldiers, so-called teams, who were to perform the funerals of the dead liquidators. All of us had to wear special suits and masks for the burials. The worst part was telling the relatives of the perished that they could not come close to the bodies of their dead. Mothers were crying because they were forbidden to hug their precious sons and husbands and to say the last "good-bye". The bodies and the coffins were highly radioactive and dangerous.

'"As soon as one of the victims had been buried in a locked and covered coffin into an unusually deep pit, the first group of young soldiers, including me, was made to rush into a special bus which took us to some kind of a sauna where we quickly took off the suits and had a shower. Our reward is ten days leave home, but I don't feel any joy about it any more."

'Three years ago I had to spend a lot of time in hospital myself with cancer and saw with my own eyes and lived through the sufferings of some of them. I knew a girl, Lida by name, 14 years old, who suffered so much because she had to wear a kerchief all the time, even when the weather was hot. She lived in Chernobyl itself and became completely bald. It is a new disease from Chernobyl and they say it has no cure. She didn't want to see her classmates; she refused to see even neighbours. She felt ashamed, but why should she?

'There were many very small children in Borovlyany hospital at that time from the contaminated zone. The majority of them had physical defects; they couldn't walk, radiation affected their bones. Their poor Mummies had to carry them in their hands, even to the building where patients got radiation treatment. When a patient gets this treatment, he or she has to lie motionless. Can a little child of three or four or five do that for four minutes? No, of course not. And because of this every day the poor little children were made to sleep with drugs. I can't imagine how their mother's hearts could bear that. When you are waiting for your turn, you can watch those who are getting the radiation treatment on a television screen. Even men couldn't stand that; their eyes were full of tears.

'Another thing that struck me there was the children's indifference to everything and everybody. When they were given toys or sweets, they wouldn't even look at them, wouldn't turn their heads. Some remained indifferent in their beds even if their mothers tried to entertain them by telling funny stories. They would lie staring into the ceiling or window. It was hard to say whether they were alive or not. Our hearts were bleeding. I can tell you frankly that we women cursed Chernobyl and those who were guilty for the lack of medicine. I'm sure that many of those little ones who died would have survived if they had been given the actual treatment they needed.

'I feel full responsibility for what I say. Once, two years ago, I was in Druzhny with a group of foreigners as a translator. Druzhny is a settlement which was erected for the evacuated families. Living conditions there were extremely bad. We visited a family of nine who lived in a flatlet of 24 square metres in total. Moreover, a girl of eleven months had cancer, her granny was in bed with cancer and her father was very ill. Our doctors couldn't cure the child, but one of the Canadians who had a daughter at home of the same age took the girl to Canada and she was cured!

'When the bus with the group of foreigners was ready to leave, many Belarussian mothers surrounded it. All of them had their sick babies in their hands. Crying, they addressed the Canadian, pleading: 'Take mine, please take mine. Cure mine. My baby is dying. Let me even not see him ever again, but let him be healthy and live in another country . . .' Can you imagine? Mothers so desperate to save their children that they would give them away to a stranger! It is terrible.

'Dear people of Ireland, thank you for your help in overcoming this horror.'

An account from a liquidator doctor

'I was conscripted on 20th March until 25th September 1988. I worked with 13 doctors and 36 women nurses in the Bragin region. Our task was to check some of the liquidators who had been working the zone for prolonged periods. The situation was dreadful. We had little or no equipment or medicine and no geiger counters. We stayed indoors for six months. We had no idea what the levels of radiation were. We knew it was high from the symptoms we found in the men and from the basic blood samples we were able to take. The men were from as far away as Siberia, none of them were allowed to contact their families, since phone calls were monitored and we were all warned about revealing where we were and what we were doing. It was a time in my life that I want to forget: The pain even now haunts me in my dreams.'

Liquidator families in Gomel

Natasha speaks: 'My husband was beautiful. He was a great sportsman, very healthy, never ill. He volunteered to work as a "liquidator" and left us in mid-april 1986. He never returned. I saw my lovely husband for the last time, standing at our door, hugging our two children, smiling. They tell me he died in 1991 of a massive heart attack at the age of 34. I don't know the truth. He never phoned from that place because of some secrecy. Some of the men told me afterwards that he had been making special dumps for things that had got radiation, like buses, tractors, bulldozers and such things. I think he got poisoned from that place. What are we to do now? No father, no husband.'

Nina speaks: 'My husband was a militiaman and was conscripted to a "top secret" job on 28th April 1986. He stayed away for one month. He returned and has never been the same. He is unable to speak about what happened during that month. He has fallen silent, as if dumb. He is in hospital most of the time. He has problems with his liver, pains in every joint. He is a changed man, always tired and distant. He never talks to me or the children any more. We are like total strangers now. I don't know what to do. The government does nothing to help us. We just get 20 cents a month compensation. Life is hell.'

Evacuee family in Gomel

Anna and her mother-in-law sat and talked to us about their life in the evacuee village of Uza. Their eyes immediately filled up with tears. Anna, ringing her handkerchief in her hands, recalled her Chernobyl story:

'My village was Slobada in the Bragin region. I first heard about Chernobyl on the 'Voice of America'. It was an alien word to me but one that would haunt me for ever. I was frightened. I had two children, aged six and nine. The militia came first with buses full of people from another village ten kilometres from Chernobyl. We had to take in these people. We felt lucky that our village was safe. But some days later they came with more buses and took us all to another village 30 kilometres from Chernobyl and forced us to leave our village. Our village had become poisoned too. They told us they would make it better and we would return three days later. But we never returned.

'My two children were taken away for something they called decontamination. I did not see them for four months. My God, can you imagine? I cry now remembering. It was terrible. My children were stolen from me. We had no news of them during that time. The separation, the not knowing, was something I can't describe to you. Then, when we were forced to leave on the buses to come to this new place – you don't know what that was like for us. For the old people. They couldn't understand what was happening. Many of the old people had to be forced out of their houses.

'My God, you should just see that beautiful place we left. In my dreams every night I return with my family to our home. The river, the trees, our garden, our house and land. This will never be my home. I cried for two years when I came here first. I felt like a dead person during those two years. Nothing is stable any more. Our place is replaced with just pipes and concrete here. Our beautiful nature. My children drank that poisoned water and they drank the milk; nobody told us not to. What have they done to us?

My children are all sick now. The people don't want us here. We are like intruders to them. It is hard to get work because people call us 'the Chernobyls'.

'My mother and father couldn't live here, so they returned. Many of the old people return. They prefer to die of radiation than to die of a broken heart. We are allowed to visit them twice a week. Everything is checked for radiation by the guards when we leave the exclusion zone. It is like going to prison, but the prison for me is on the outside.'

'On the "Day of the Dead" (a national day of mourning) they allow us home for a couple of hours. We don't see each other for the tears. It is terrible. Our houses are all looted. They have even ripped out our floorboards and sold them. All our things are gone. We have lost everything. Can you imagine – they even took the photograph of Mama. Why? I don't know anything any more.'

Anna's mother-in-law told us: 'When I return on the "Day of the Dead", I have no feelings, just tears. I can't put all the tears into words. It was my birthplace. Our village was everything: the forest, the river, the sun. I don't recognize anyone any more. There are no single memories, just all these years flashing by my eyes. Chernobyl means death.'

Children's voices

These accounts were taped during the visit of Chernobyl children to Ireland in the summer of 1994.

Elena Thiteneva, aged 14: 'When the accident happened, I was five. We used to live in a village near Khoiniki. I remember the great horror that my parents and our relatives felt. They said that there were many more victims than had been announced. We were evacuated to the Vitebsk region. We were given milk free of charge for three months. After evacuation we were taken to hospital. It was very bad there. Mothers cried because they didn't want us to stay without them. Many of them stayed in hiding places to see us. I spent four weeks in quarantine. I suffered from stomach disturbances and vomiting. My appetite disappeared. My brother suffered from heavy headaches. I have to go to hospital every year.'

Sergei Kakora, aged 14: 'I remember very clearly that on one

April day in 1986 all of a sudden there was a violent dust storm. The wind was carrying heavy, dark, black clouds. Everyone started to protect their mouths and eyes. The next day we got to hear that the reactor had blown up. I remember that my throat became hoarse and I coughed all the time. Later we were evacuated. The rescue parties came as soon as the fire at the reactor was put out. Nobody was told that they were leaving their places for ever. We left our houses unlocked, leaving everything behind. I remember the great shock my grandmother had when she had to leave all the poultry, cattle and dogs behind to be shot by the police. It was clear that we didn't understand the danger, we simply couldn't believe in that invisible death. I felt very bad, my blood was bad. I have annual treatment. Now it is a little better. My father is a driver. In 1986 he was a liquidator. He used to carry radioactive concrete blocks for the shell over the reactor. Nowadays he suffers great problems.'

Svetlana Petrachenko, aged 12: 'We lived in the village of Tabeni, not far from the zone, maybe 30 kilometres. Our family was not evacuated. Only six of us were taken for three months to the Gomel region. My youngest brother was born after the accident. He was very thin, weak and pale and he couldn't suck well. Then we went back and in only one year three of the children were taken away; in another year I was evacuated as well. I remember that I was sick all the time. My granny cried very much. She refused to go and stayed in the village. Later my grandfather died of radiation cancer. A lot of people, including our relatives, died of it.'

Vasily Thloba, aged 10: 'I was evacuated from a village four years after the explosion. My parents wanted to go, but my grandparents didn't. They cried a lot. When I was three, my health began to deteriorate. I started vomiting and had severe headaches. The doctors gave me injections all the time. My eyes were very bad. I was sent to Leningrad to a special hospital for a month. After a month's treatment, I felt better, but I still suffer often.'

Nicholai Borodko, aged 8: 'We lived in the village of Pusichi near Gomel. Later we were evacuated to Soligorsk, but my grandparents refused to go and now they still live there. My mother (aged 35) is very ill. She's got lung disease and now is an invalid. She stays at home, can't work even about the house and suffers from suffocations.'

Julia Philipenko, aged 14: 'We were evacuated to Druzhny. I was six. My parents rushed to my kindergarten and took me home and I was forbidden to go out. I feel fear and pity. I hate being ill. I have a sick heart, thyroid and tonsils. My mother's eyes were full of tears when I was six.'

Olga Gapeyeva, aged 12: 'My parents are divorced since the accident. We were evacuated to Minsk. The reactor brought grief and damage. Something extremely harmful polluted our country. Many children are born with defects. A lot of mothers cry and never smile. I used to cry. I feel compassion for all the people of my village, Vetka. I remember my mother seized me and took me to another village when I was four.'

Marina Buntina, aged 10: 'I don't remember the accident. I know that Chernobyl is war. Many people are wounded. I suffer from my thyroid.'

Svetlana Khalyukova, aged 12: 'I suffer from thyroid problems and I am an evacuee. We were not allowed to drink milk. We suffer. I am angry with the people who built this reactor. If the reactor hadn't exploded, I wouldn't have to leave my mother every summer.'

Nickolai Kuleshov, aged 13: 'I lived in the country and my father was a liquidator. I think that we must not build atomic power stations, especially if we can't do it properly. I am very sorry because I had to part with my friends. Many people of my village are continuing to die. I remember that on that very day of Chernobyl, we were gathering cherries and all of a sudden a very, very strong wind blew and a lot of bright red clouds appeared in the sky. We got frightened and ran into the house.'

Vladimir Chidakov, aged 9: 'I still live in the most contaminated zone waiting to be evacuated. I know this because after the explosion I had to stay in hospital, and last year I didn't go to school at all. I hate being blood-tested all the time.'

Andrei Areshchenko, aged 13: 'I live in the contaminated zone and suffer with my thyroid. We are not allowed to eat fish from our rivers or vegetables from our own gardens. I am very sorry. I remember Chernobyl. I was outdoors playing in the playground when suddenly a strong wind began blowing and my mother made me go into the house and didn't let me leave.'

Soura Efimovich, aged 11: 'I know that it is forbidden to eat berries which grow in our forest.'

Sergei Kopysev, aged 14: 'My sister tells me not to be barefoot. It's dangerous.'

Vica Burak, aged 8: 'I know that I live in a radioactive zone and we will not be evacuated. I am afraid that something will happen to me.'

Dima Batura, aged 9: 'I know that it is not allowed to swim in our rivers.'

Helen Protchenko, aged 11: 'Mother tells me that radiation is an invisible enemy; that's why it's very dangerous.'

Helen Klyga, aged 11: 'My granny doesn't allow me to go to the forest any more to gather berries and mushrooms.'

Vadim Kalykhan, aged 13: 'We know that we are staying in Ireland because of the bad environment in the Gomel region. Here it is safe to play and walk freely on the grass, in the streets, in the playgrounds. At home our parents and teachers forbid us to go out. They say it might influence our health badly.'

Kate Zesulina and Alina Maslova, aged 10 and 12: 'Our parents and relatives talk a lot about the radiation: what we should and should not eat, because in Belarus we eat vegetables and fruit which were grown in the contaminated zones. They remember the time when they could pick mushrooms and berries in the forest; it was before the explosion. Now, when we buy something, we must check it at the special radiation control station. And our parents say that they are tired of thinking all the time about the radiation. That is why they don't ask any longer if the food is from strongly contaminated areas or not. We just eat it now.'

Inna Melnikova, aged 10: 'My mother and my grandparents worry about my health. They say I might have enjoyed better health if there hadn't been that radiation. I feel ill very often, especially in winter and spring. I remember that my mother couldn't find the medicine which had been prescribed for me by a doctor. My mother told me that our vitamins were not so good as those from abroad. That is why I am glad to be in Ireland. We eat tasty things here and take vitamins. My mother couldn't buy bananas and other fruit for me because they are so expensive. Here I have plenty and I feel better.'

Katia, aged 10: 'At home I vomit and get headaches. In Ireland I am not sick and the air is safe.'

Stories such as these were told to us as the days of the children's visit went by. Little by little, their own stories began to unfold, the true scale of their hurt becoming more apparent all the time.

What we were not prepared for was how much we would grow to love the children! They swept us off our feet and strong bonding happened between the families and the children. They are extremely charismatic and the gift they have given to us is quite beyond understanding in words. It is both an honour and a privilege to have had them enter our lives even for such a short time. The children had an understanding of their situation and somehow managed constantly to transform the horror of their lives and celebrated daily what life they had left. They are an example to us all.

8

The Day of the Dead

WE ARRIVED IN the city of Gomel to film the banned protest rally which had been organized for the seventh anniversary of the accident. Gomel is the medical centre in one of the most seriously contaminated regions. The rally was poorly attended because people feared the repercussions of being seen at it. Only the old and the brave took part and marched the streets with heads held high in defiance of the strong police presence. I was supposed to remain an impartial observer, but I couldn't. I ran to join the start to the protest. Someone handed me a cotton vest that said 'Chernobyl . . . Our Pain'. I wore it as a gesture of solidarity. I walked alongside Galina Artyomenko, who told me how she had already lost one of her children to radiation and was herself seriously ill.

Singlehandedly Galina had organized this march and told me she would no longer be rendered silent by fear of the authorities. She had nothing left to lose. When we arrived at the meeting point of the rally, speeches began and the anger felt by the crowd was transferred into the burning of an effigy of the mayor of Gomel, who at the height of the radiation cloud over Gomel ordered the citizens of the city to attend the open-air May Day parade. Many people participated out of fear and received very high doses of radiation. It was discovered afterwards that the mayor and his family had secretly left for the safety of Moscow days before the parade.

During the filming that afternoon, our producer, Liam, had become friendly with a seven-year-old girl called Alicia. Out of their initial interplay of laughing and gestures came a very special story that ended up becoming a part of the documentary. Alicia had been born in the radiation zone after the accident. She had been abandoned in a deserted area, where she was found by the police, who brought her to an orphanage. A journalist called Larissa Gramatchikova from Gomel had been writing a story on the ever-increasing numbers of abandoned children, and came across Alicia. She fell in love with her and adopted her. Larissa told us that, in a strange way, Chernobyl had brought her happiness.

That evening the film crew gathered together in Ali's and my room to hold our own Chernobyl remembrance ceremony. Earlier in the day Dónal, Ali and I had visited a church and had bought 14 blessed candles. We held a lighted candle as we each fell silent, none of us yet having the courage or trust to express our emotions or fears about what we were experiencing. This trust, when it eventually came, bonded the group into a powerful force in the making of what became a very special 'witness'.

The following morning we visited a maternity ward in Gomel Hospital. I can still remember the sense of fear and despair expressed by the mothers as they waited with anxiety for the birth of their babies, anxiety that is reflected in the 50% drop in birth-rates in the zone area, as mothers are afraid to give birth. The nurse who talked with us spoke about the 300% increase in hypoxia (oxygen starvation of the womb). She told us about the birth of 'lightweight' babies of 500 grams and the difficulties they had in sustaining these little lives because they lack enough incubators and medicine. One little baby we filmed that day nearly died hours after we had filmed her laboured breathing.

Many of the women we spoke to told us they were unable to feed their babies because their own milk had dried up. There is little access to baby food and it is only available to those who can afford to buy it on the black market. For those who can still breast-feed, there are severe restrictions and monitoring because their breast-milk can be radioactive. There is also an increase of pathology and complications during labour. Many women are so traumatized that they cannot carry their babies full-term and give birth prematurely.

Leaving the hospital gave us personal relief, but not for long. We went on to visit an old sanatorium for children outside Gomel, which houses hundreds of children from the heavily contaminated regions for two-month periods of respite. The benefit of these short stays is to help the immune system to rest and recover, and then the children must return to the zone. Then the cycle starts again. We walked around the wards, which were crammed with beds. Pale, wan, fragile children were lying in their beds, resting. The more curious and energetic crowded around us, all chattering together. Dr Alexander Stepanenko explained that he had little medicine and no multivitamins. He told us that he catered for over 2,000 children a year from the Gomel district. He had a six-month waiting list which was growing daily. We promised to do what we could to help on our return to Ireland.

We continued that day with a visit to a special school for Chernobyl children who had to have six diseases before they could be accepted as a student. In the course of our preliminary conversations we asked the school principal if he had a geiger counter in order to monitor the children's radiation exposure on a daily basis. He said, 'I have one with no battery. I don't need it anymore. We already know that we are radioactive, so why alarm the children with the constant screeching of a radiation machine? The children have enough to cope with. They already feel like they are under siege by radiation. We will not add to their already great alarm.'

Each year, one week after Easter, there is a day of national mourning in Belarus, 'The Day of the Dead'. On this day thousands of evacuees are allowed, under military escort, to return to grieve and mourn at the graves of their loved ones. We filmed this poignant day in the deserted village of Lipa, not far from Gomel.

Getting permission to participate in and film this day proved to be a major bureaucratic ordeal. Several times before we entered the exclusion zone we felt that permission was going to be withdrawn. We played a tightrope waltz with officials who wanted to deny the extent of the problem and yet knew that the only solution for the problem lay in a response from the international community. Having being pushed from pillar to post, we finally found ourselves at the exclusion zone fence. This area is policed by a special force who are fully armed and have the right to shoot on sight within the exclusion zones. We stood and looked over the fence. We saw our first deserted village, Lipa. It once housed several hundred families. The evacuations took place here five years after the accident. Five years too late.

The crew had met the night before and we decided that we could not risk frightening the evacuees by wearing our special protective clothing. Instead, we would wear disposable clothes which would have to be burned or buried on our return to Gomel. The crew stood watching and filming the evacuees as they arrived by bus and car to re-enter the village of their ancestors. The guard swung open the gate, a gate which carried a special radiation sign with the words in Cyrillic, 'STOP, do not enter. Forbidden radiation zone. No fishing, farming, grazing of cattle. No picking of mushrooms or berries.' The people entered the outskirts of their village under the strict eye of the guards.

Finally our turn came. Under armed escort we entered the village. Silence descended. Everything and nothing changed. As we drove down the main village street, we looked and saw the little timber houses, with the traditional seat for the old people outside each house; the ornate drinking wells; a house with washing still on the line, too radioactive to be taken down; a child's bicycle up against the fence of a house, a doll sat in the window staring. An eerie feeling like that evoked by the Hitchcock movie *The Birds* crept over me.

In the distance we saw a cluster of trees on a hill. Our guide told us that this was the traditional place in every village for the graveyard. It is on a height so that the dead can watch, listen to and be a part of what happens in the village below. Droves of people covered the pathway up the hill, slowly winding their way to their ancient sacred burial grounds. We parked and prepared our equipment, conscious that we must be very obvious to the people around the graveyard. We anxiously asked the people for permission to film and interview. We were much relieved by the welcome we received.

As unobtrusively as possible, I started my job of taking geiger-counter readings every ten minutes. Without wanting to alarm the evacuees, I wrote down each reading and showed it to the crew. We knew that we were on borrowed time. We couldn't stay in this highly radioactive area for too long without running a very serious personal risk. I continued to monitor for the next four hours. With each reading, I got more anxious and constantly added up the total dosage to ensure that we didn't over-expose ourselves.

We stood and watched as the village people recongregated, surrounded by an armed guard. They embraced each other, cried with each other over the lives they had had to leave behind, and yet celebrated that they were still alive. Families encircled their family grave. They laid clothes over the grave mound and shared a meal. At the head of the grave a dish with a little bread, a glass of vodka and some hard-boiled eggs were left to be symbolically shared with the spirit of the dead relative. I found this gathering very moving and reminiscent of similar traditions in Ireland. I envied their strong connection with their dead, a connection that is almost lost in the Western 'developed' world. We discovered the importance of old people to all Belarussians. The extended family is everything, and the old people are treated with enormous respect. Not to be able to visit the graves of their loved ones is a loss that cannot be quantified for Belarussians. It is as if a part of their very heart is wrenched from them. Old people told us about the terror of being evacuated and the loneliness they now feel in being separated from their community.

I saw one old woman banging her head against the gravestone of her son who died in 1986. She cried out her grief. Looking around the graves, I was struck by how many of them are dated 1987, 1988. A man pointed to the land of his forefathers that he too had once farmed. He wished that some day he could return behind his horse and plough to bring life to these fields again – a wish that will never come true, as they are poisoned with radiation.

While the guards were preoccupied, one old woman, Tanya, secretly brought us to her home. We walked with her through the rooms, now left to rot in the house she had worked so hard to maintain. She pointed to the corner where her bed used to be, the corner where the kitchen dresser had stood for decades. Tanya talked about how she was forever 'rooted like a tree' to the earth of her ancestors, but now she was 'withering away and dying'. She told us the awfulness she felt at the finality of the realization that she would not be able to return. She looked around her little farmyard, shaking her head in disbelief. 'We didn't just lose our village, we lost a life. Chernobyl is like a big stone in my heart, always there, always heavy.'

We found a family in hiding in this village. When we asked why they were staying in the world's most radioactive environment, the man knelt on the ground, picked up some earth and, with tears running down his face, kissed it and told us: 'This earth is sacred, the earth of my ancestors; this earth is my soul; take me from the earth and you take my soul.'

Ali and I walked around the dead village to find further places for our cameraman to film. What a strange feeling it was to 'invade' the privacy of someone's home, to see all their personal things, to know the kind of life they had. Standing in someone's apple garden, we switched on the geiger counter. We both stared at the reading. The counter had jumped enormously since our previous reading five minutes earlier. Holding our breath, we ran from that deceptively lovely garden and found a safer place in the garden next door. We were afraid to go indoors, although psychologically we thought we would be safer. We had read only the previous night how the small, innocent, timber houses had absorbed huge doses of radiation, and for those who had lived in them it had been like living inside 'mini reactors'. We ran to the dirt road, more exposed but a little safer. For the first time, we acknowledged each other's fear. What we had just experienced was a phenomenon known as 'spotty contamination'. These 'hot spots' are everywhere, invisible except to the sensitivity of a geiger counter. It is apparently impossible to decontaminate such patches of heavy contamination. We told the rest of the crew what had happened. There was a spurt to finish what filming and sound-tracking still needed to be done.

Leaving Lipa, I began to withdraw into myself. We left the zone and within minutes came to a village identical to the one we had just left. It was the same except for one thing: this village had life. Children played on the dust road; old people chatted outside their homes, drinking tea and smoking pipes; hens pecked around the grassy verges. I saw a woman hanging washing on the line; I thought of the washing on the line in Lipa. I saw a little girl stroking the doll in her arms; I flashed back to the doll in the window. I couldn't stop my tears flowing at the unfairness and suffering of it all. I cried for myself too. The others pretended that they didn't notice, but they knew that my tears were for them too.

We journeyed from Gomel through many towns and villages and eventually stopped to film a Russian Orthodox ceremony at Soligorsk. This town is very special to Ireland because we have 'adopted' two local orphanages, along with the hospital, as part of our holiday and medical aid programme.

The church was adorned with beautiful icons and we saw people receiving public confession. The ceremony, conducted by six priests, had lasted for several hours. The church was packed and the ceremony was to 'give thanks' to Ireland for all that we had done. Despite the fact that none of us knew a word of Russian, we fully understood the significance of what was taking place, both by the depth of emotion being expressed and by the symbolism. As each of the priests spoke, they cried, both for the children and for the death of their country. The chief priest turned and said through our interpreter Natasha, 'The people of Ireland are not only saving the lives of our children, but you are offering them hope to live.' The specialness of this tribute was continued through a beautiful ceremony of light. The Chernobyl children who had been to Ireland came to the altar and each lit a candle as a symbol of hope for the future.

After the ceremony we met the children's parents at a party held in our honour. It was a night of great laughter as well as tears. While working in Belarus I went through the whole gamut of emotions, constantly swinging from great sadness to feelings of joy and fun.

Continuing on our journey, we visited small rural towns and villages in the non-compulsory radiation zone (the radioactive area in which people were not subject to enforced evacuation). The people we met in the towns and villages were full of heart and feeling. Their world is one that we in the West have almost lost, and in a sense we gained access to that 'lost world' when we immersed ourselves in village life.

I particularly enjoyed visiting the schools. I remember one in a place called Varovichi which was attended by 600 children, even though it had been built for only 100. The teachers had to work in two shifts for no extra pay. They began at 8 a.m. and finished at 8 p.m., working with two groups of 300 children. Despite the overcrowding, the school was full of energy and vitality. All the students and their teachers and parents came to greet us. We felt like royalty! Afterwards we discovered the reason for the fuss. We were the first foreigners the children or the adults had ever seen. One teacher came up to us, touched my sleeve and said, 'I don't believe it! I am touching a real foreigner! And it's lovely!'

Afterwards, seated around a table having cups of Russian tea with the teachers, we talked excitedly to them about our impressions of their country, about politics and the West. We even tried a few jokes. We asked them many questions about the possibility of the opposition party, the Belarussian People's Popular Front, getting into power and bringing about genuine change in the country. In the teachers' response we heard again the opinion that 'Nothing will change', or 'Nothing will make a difference.'

This terrible resignation and acceptance of their situation deeply disturbed all of us. So whenever we got the opportunity we tried to convince our Belarussian friends to have faith in their own ability to organize themselves at a community level and to bring about change politically, economically and socially. The teachers argued strongly that 'It is not possible to bring about change.' Giving example after example, including the one of Nelson Mandela and South Africa, we tried to encourage our new friends into believing enough in themselves to take action against the injustice of their lives.

Personal political power is unknown in their culture, and we were talking alien ideas to them, but none the less the seeds of new thinking were sown. We hope that in the years to come we shall see ordinary people in Belarus taking charge of their lives and bringing about significant structural changes in their country.

When I asked them for their thoughts on Chernobyl, I found that their way of coping with the fact that they were living, sleeping, eating and drinking in a radiation zone was to go into denial. It reminded me of what the Australian doctor and anti-nuclear campaigner Helen Caldicott refers to as 'psychic numbing', a condition whereby some people lull themselves into believing the opposite of what is true in order to protect themselves from reality. Not only are many of the people affected by Chernobyl suffering from this condition, but also sometimes I believe that the whole world is suffering from an epidemic of 'numbing psychosis', and it is time that we woke up. The teachers constantly referred to the zones as if they were somewhere else, not here but over there, even though in the next breath they would mention how they are restricted from eating mushrooms and berries grown in their locality. It was only a 'precaution', they told us, and was not an acknowledgement that they lived in the zone themselves.

9

Sanity on the edge

W<small>E ARRIVED AT</small> the edge of the 'purple zone' to spend the next four days in the dreaded area that we had only read about in our research. This is the area of massive contamination. It is an area in which movement is severely restricted. There is no place, past or present, with which one could compare it. We decided to stay in the village of Khoniki, which is in the Non-Compulsory Evacuation Area. This was a new zone that none of us had ever heard of, as it had only recently been implemented. This meant that the radiation zones now stretched for a total of 70 kilometres from Chernobyl.

Anyone who can afford to or who has some place else to go has left. When we arrived in Khoniki, it was only partially inhabited. First of all we had to check in with the local mayor. He was a 'tough' man about whom we had been advised in advance. This was the man we must convince to allow us to film in the exclusion zone and in the other surrounding villages. Liam, Gerry and I were sent as the delegation to represent our case. We found the mayor exactly as he had been described. Getting the formalities over with quickly, we tried to impress upon him the importance of our documentary to his country. He wore an undisguised look of cynicism the whole time and clearly told us that he had no time for foreign film-makers.

We started again. This time I tried to impress him with my international political and peace connections, slightly exaggerating them where possible. Bingo! When I mentioned the Board of Directors of the International Peace Bureau in Geneva, which has consultative status to UNISOC, he started to get impressed. I tried to engage him with strong eye contact and seriously told him that he was looking at three 'very important people'. We eventually made a deal with him which kept him satisfied, and we got to make our film. The deal included medical aid for the local hospital and taking 20 local children to Ireland for rest and recuperation. Not a bad deal, considering we would have made this offer anyway!

However, there was still one hurdle. The mayor was not the overall 'boss' of the exclusion zone. There was another man whom we had to meet, and he had total control and power over where we could go and what we could film. Our hearts sank slightly, but we believed that we could convince him. The meeting was set for 8 p.m. that evening. Liam, Gerry and I were delegated to go.

We returned to tell the rest of the crew what had happened, and we proceeded to what we thought was the local hotel. The place that was to be our home for the next four days turned out to be some kind of brothel with 'business' going on day and night! The building was dilapidated and there was nothing whatsoever about it inside or outside that resembled even the worst hotel you could ever imagine! Somehow it seemed appropriate for where we were and what we were doing, so we didn't get too bothered when we turned on the tap and found that the water was dark brown and freezing cold, or that there were only two toilets. To enter these you needed rubber boots on your feet, a strong stomach and a large peg on your nose! We didn't bother to ask about a shower or bath!

On our first night there we discovered that we were 'locked up'. There was no way of getting in or out of the building. We were very alarmed by this and the following morning demanded an explanation from the local authorities, who promptly informed us that it was 'for your own good'. When pressed further, we discovered that wild animals roamed from area to area and were highly radioactive. On the evening in question a herd of wild pigs entered the village and had to be shot by the police. When examined for radioactivity, they were found to be 1,000% above acceptable levels. After that explanation, we had no problem with being 'locked up'!

Since we were in a restricted area, we had brought our own food and water with us and a small electric ring, so that at least we could boil up water to make some instant soup. On our first night in the world's most radioactive environment we delegated Dónal and Ali to cook us some dinner. Liam and I left to find the 'all-powerful' man who would decide the fate of the documentary. We found him living in squalid conditions. He was agitated and appeared cross. Liam and I had worked out our strategy, and we started to speak. He listened impassively. We again had to pull out all the impressive titles and connections, and things started to improve slightly. At this stage we had been there for about two hours. Liam and I were afraid to show our eagerness, and continued to outline what we needed to do in order to make the 'best documentary in the world' about Chernobyl.

The man was dishevelled and his apartment was a reflection of his physical state. But when it came to expertise on Chernobyl, he was a fountain of information and he told us things we had not heard previously. This man was the king of the radioactive zone, all-powerful in determining what happened within this 'no man's land'. We talked about going to the zone as if it were a new, strange and untamed world, belonging to him.

He talked about the problems with the thousands of deserted villages all around the zone. They looked dead, but the radiation would not stay dead or buried. Much of the contaminated debris was buried in shallow graves, he told us, which were becoming more and more exposed and causing huge new problems as a new source of contamination. These graves included everything from buried tanks and fire engines to concrete from buildings. There were some 800 such primitive disposal sites scattered around the area.

These dumps are a nightmare source of contamination, not only through the soil and air, but through the water. The possibility of contamination of the water table for 40 million people in the Ukraine is now becoming a very serious threat. These are the same waters that run into the Dnieper river, which flows to the Black Sea. The tributary rivers that eventually feed the Dnieper all come through the 'Purple Zone'. There is no escape from the radiation. As a result, the Dnieper has already become the world's most radioactive river.

In order to prevent the radioactivity from the dumps getting into the water table, they have built several underground dams to contain the contaminated water. But this in turn has caused the water table levels to rise. In places the water has risen by a metre and a half, and in some places up to three metres. There is a big fear concerning Plutonium 239, as it seems to have converted into liquid form. If it mixes with the natural water table serious contamination of the drinking water of the Ukraine could result.

One of the problems which the 'king of the zone' identified was that of trying to keep the people still living in villages close to the exclusion zone from entering the zone and doing what they've been doing for generations: hunting, fishing, picking berries and mushrooms, swimming and grazing cattle. These activities are banned, and part of the function of the 'king' was to rigidly police the area. His men have the right to shoot or imprison any 'culprits' breaking the law.

Part of the role of his special police force is to patrol and monitor the zone during the summertime. During the intensely hot summers, part of their monitoring includes watching out for forest and bush fires which further spread the radioactivity. This has become a major dilemma and one not predicted by the scientists. His team have found alarming amounts of strontium 90 and caesium 137 that have been blown and scattered across a vast area, thus causing recontamination of the soil, air and water. This problem has made the evacuations a nightmare, as they find that some of the areas where new villages have been built for evacuees are now more radioactive than the areas they previously lived in.

The 'king' seemed relieved to be able to talk to us, and once he realized that we could be trusted he told us yet more about the crises he had to deal with. Another major, unforseen problem is the movement of all kinds of wild animals in and out of the zone. Barbed wire and 'keep out' signs mean nothing to them. No one had predicted the problems that would arise in the Purple Zone once the natural culling process from hunting had stopped. Now his 300-strong police force must hunt down the animals and shoot them. But still the animals continue to procreate and carry the radiation way beyond the zone. Hedgehogs, according to the police, are the worst animal source of contamination. Local villagers around the zone who have little access to good meat also hunt the animals, even though it is now prohibited, so the nightmare chain of contamination continues.

He laughed every so often. I'm not sure if the laugh was from despair or from some 'kick' he got from his bizarre job. He hummed and hawed about our requests to film and smoked another cigarette. He thought in silence. We held our breath. I took a furtive look around his one-roomed apartment. The walls were covered in soft-porn posters. The window was broken. A baby's cot sat in the corner. Finally, he spoke and, yes, he agreed to give permission. But he insisted that to 'seal' the deal we must have a drink with him. With vodka in jam-jars we drank to each other's health. Finally we left and returned to freshly made vegetable soup, stale bread, tins of tuna fish in a spicy sauce, wet cheddar cheese and the last bars of chocolate. Everyone celebrated with relief. We sat and ate while we planned our next visit to the deserted villages in the area.

We now had to be self-sufficient for food and water, and we agreed each morning on how much water we could each drink. What had seemed like a massive quantity of water when we had checked it in at Shannon Airport had by now diminished at a fast pace. Our food boxes had also disappeared, and agreement was made as to how much we could eat per day. We were a surprisingly democratic group and arrived at all major decisions by consensus. Well, that's a slight exaggeration! There were moments of tension as there were disagreements about who and what should be filmed, but generally speaking we worked well as a team and learned to trust and rely on each other's judgements and expertise more and more.

The following morning everyone congregated in the room which Ali and I were sharing, and we boiled up the water in a traditional samovar (which leaked all the time!) and had more wet cheese and stale bread. Fully fortified for the day, we piled into our van and were taken by local people to the first deserted village, just a short distance from Khoniki town.

We arrived in Mikulvichi, a handsome village with very ornate and elaborate timberwork on the houses. The sun was shining. It was a beautiful, innocent spring day. Everything appeared normal until you looked around and noticed that there were no people on the streets, no children playing. Total silence. Strange, strange feelings. To fill the gulf of silence, we talked extra loudly, cracked a couple of jokes. Looking around the place, it seemed like the most inviting spot you could find to spend some time in.

We started to move out and around the houses and much to our surprise, we discovered that not everyone had been evacuated. We met a family living together as best they could. We found an old man living by himself, still awaiting evacuation seven years later. He was thrilled with such lively foreign company and invited us into his little house. Immediately the bottle of vodka appeared and together with our translator, he made us some scrambled eggs. Despite our agreements about 'no food in the zone', we knew that this was a special occasion for him and we ate as much as we could and washed it quickly down with a glass of vodka. We consoled ourselves by remembering the doctor's words in Gomel: 'Vodka helps to reduce the radiation.' Just in case there was any truth in this theory, we drank it in large gulps! The old man told us about his life, a life that had been very tough even without Chernobyl. It included a ten-year period in Siberia for 'reasons unspecified'.

I felt very sad in this village; it had a special feel to it. Apart from a few old people and the family we met, the village was empty and silent. One strange sight in the village, and in all the others we were yet to see, was the perfect new tarmac roads. They had been made since the accident to replace the dirt roads and so to try to keep the radioactivity down. Roads that will never be used by anyone. Later it was to get even more strange, when we saw trucks patrolling the zone, spraying the verges with water in an attempt to dampen down the radioactivity.

I wanted to scream out and try and bring life and laughter back to the place. Just as I was thinking these thoughts, Isobel and Dónal looked at me, and I knew we were having the same thoughts. What could we do? We looked around and saw that the old man we had spoken to had a small horse and cart tied up by his gate, and we asked if we could borrow it.

None of us had any experience in how to drive a horse and cart. Dónal assured us that he knew, but I somehow had my doubts! We jumped up on the cart and with a yelp and a yahoo we went galloping up and down the unused streets of Mikulvichi, scream-ing and singing all the way! The old man was delighted. He knew why we needed to do it. He lived his life with the empty, barren village and missed all the obvious signs of human life. For some fleeting seconds we roared out our anger and sorrow for what had been done to these people.

That was the day of 'nuclear enlightenment', a day when the reality started to sink deeper and deeper into our very souls. I remembered the words of Oppenheimer, one of the key scientists working on the Manhattan Project, when he spoke about his own personal moment of understanding when he fully appreciated the destructive power which had been unleashed in 1945. As he stood looking at the mushroom cloud caused by the first nuclear bomb test in the Nevada desert, he said, 'Some of us laughed, some of us cried, some of us fell silent. I was reminded of the Hindu scripture, "I am become death, destroyer of worlds."' As I stood in that village, witnessing the reality of his words all around me, my sadness deepened.

We were registering shock after shock, but were unable to fully comprehend or verbalize it. We were between worlds, verging at times on the crazy. Later that day, as the lads were setting up camera for some shots of radiation-poisoned fields, the three 'girls' – Ali, Isobel and I – were trying to cope with what we were surrounded by, and we started to hum and make up songs and tunes. In between taking geiger counter readings, we formed 'The Chernobylettes', the only all women's song and dance act to come out of Chernobyl! Well, if we hadn't laughed we would have cried.

On our way back from filming that afternoon we had to stop to eat some more tuna fish and, just for variety, some cream crackers, and our dilemma was where we would stop to eat! We were in the radiation zone, for God's sake! When I look back on it I shudder at how we learned to adjust to our strange situation. Our dilemma was simply solved by sending three of us in different directions, each armed with a geiger counter, and wherever we got the lowest reading, that would be the spot for the picnic. Hard to imagine, but that's what we did, and we had a lovely time, laughing and joking all the way.

On our journey back to Khoniki our driver took us to what looked like a huge warehouse. When we asked why he had stopped he said that he thought we would be interested in filming it because it was the nuclear decontamination centre for the area. This was the place where they brought the buses, tanks, bicycles and cars to be washed down with special chemicals to make them 'safe'. Being the curious kind of bunch we were, out we got ready to film. The place was locked, but someone who will remain nameless broke in! We reckoned that it wasn't exactly breaking in because there would never be anyone in the area again, so we didn't feel so bad. We squeezed in the door and suddenly what seemed like thousands of pigeons descended down from the rafters. Their flapping wings gave an eerie effect to the place. We worked silently, imagining what it must have been like during the decontamination process: the sounds of people shouting in panic to have their vehicles sprayed; the sounds of engines and machinery roaring. Now this place was a silent monument.

Our driver, Kostya, was also anxious for us to visit a sweet factory which was still producing sweets which were eaten by the entire population of Belarus. It was situated on the edge of the 'Purple Zone'. The factory used only local produce, including the milk. We were astounded by this story and discussed the possibility of increasing our time in the zone to pursue it. As our time was practically measured down to the last minute in this area, we had to decline the possibility of unfolding yet another nightmare. The destructive path of Chernobyl is a labyrinth, tangled and never-ending.

The following morning we went to visit the local primary school in Khoniki to get an understanding of what school life was like in the middle of all this craziness. What did we find? More craziness! We discovered that the first lesson for all little children every day was one to ensure that they would not forget their radioactive environment and would always observe the restrictions in their lives. The teacher went through a list of questions such as 'What is radiation? Where is the radiation? Why is it dangerous? What is strontium, plutonium, uranium, caesium?' A child in the middle of the class responded, 'It's in the trees and in the grass.' A boy at the back said, 'It's in the streams and rivers.' My God, what are we teaching our children? Listening to the teacher and the children's response, I was almost overwhelmed by the injustice of such innocents having their most precious childhood years marred by radioactivity. The teachers told us how the children's lives were restricted by a series of bans. They couldn't walk in the forests, swim in the streams or pick wild flowers and berries. Their lives revolved around radiation.

By this time we had become the local curiosity of the town, and every time we returned, gangs of little children would congregate around the van. They brought us little gifts which we were sure had been 'borrowed' from their mothers and fathers, as they had a somewhat 'worn' look about them! We in turn gave them gifts of chocolates and sweets. We became somewhat 'settled' in this strange place and developed a sort of attachment even to the odd 'hotel' where we were staying. The human capacity to adjust to even the most 'off-the-wall' situation never ceases to amaze me!

This same group of poor children caused us great alarm when we returned to our accommodation, having filmed in a highly radioactive area. We had taken the precaution of wearing our radiation dust suits and masks and had all our gear packed in plastic bags to be disposed of by our driver, who was en route to having our vehicle decontaminated. Unfortunately he didn't tell us that his idea of 'safe disposal' was a rubbish heap behind our building. As we were dressing into clean clothes Dónal the cameraman looked out the window and shouted with alarm. The children had found the radioactive suits and masks and were wearing them and playing around in the yard. Dónal's shout alerted the rest of the crew. Gerry jumped out of the window of the two-storey building. Liam and Dan went flying down the stars. Ali, Isobel and I stared out the window in dismay. The children were thrilled with what they thought was a game of 'chase', and it took quite some time before the suits were recovered. We decided that we could not leave the bags of suits in the open and took the decision, rightly or wrongly, to burn the gear. It was a strange ritual that followed. Not only did we have to burn the suits and masks but also all the personal clothing, underwear and footwear that we had worn during the past few days. We formed a relay line. Ali stood at the bedroom window and tossed out the bags one by one to Dan and Gerry. Liam and Dónal guarded the fire. Isobel and I watched the children. We were all silent. We were aware of the dangers attached to burning the radioactive clothes, but we felt we had little choice.

Later the same day we went in search of a deserted village that we had heard about where some of the old former residents had returned. The authorities had decided to leave them in peace because of their age. The trauma of evacuation had proved to be too much to suffer for many of the old people. Throughout our days within the 'non compulsory exclusion zone' we found old people who had returned to hide in their former homes, to die with dignity on the land of their forefathers. The authorities turn a 'blind eye' to them, as they recognize the difficulties which these peasant people experience in the alien environment of a city.

The village we arrived in was called Tulgovichi. Almost all the houses were empty and overgrown, but we soon picked out the couple of occupied ones and with relief we entered the gardens to talk to the old people. Four of them were out working in bare feet. Two men were working the horse and plough, while two women followed along, dropping in seed potatoes.

Unfortunately for me, this was one of the days when I became violently ill. I hoped it was a tummy bug and not radiation poisoning. I was unable to stop vomiting. The lads were busy filming the farming activities while I ran from garden to garden, trying to be sick as discretely as possible. There was a joke in all of this! While I was busy vomiting, Ali and Isobel, who were minding me, said that I was lucky the place was deserted, as I could choose a different garden to be ill in every time! Two of the old women heard the noises I was making, as there was nothing else to break the silence. They quietly offered me some strong tea. I didn't want to take it, but neither did I want to cause insult, so I gingerly sampled the tea made with water from their well. The tea didn't stay with me either, and I had to run to yet another deserted garden! Definitely this was not my day! Let's hope it was the tuna fish that was 'talking' to me and not the dreaded 'R' word!

Having slept off whatever it was, I was fit and ready for work the next morning. It was to be a day that would be etched for ever on all of our memories! We went to the local registry office to film a wedding. We were trying to capture all the events in the 'ordinary' people's lives, and how they had to try and live on, despite their circumstances. The bride, like all brides, was beautiful, and after a very quick ceremony we followed the wedding party to film the reception in the bride's back garden. It was a terrific affair, with people, children, dogs, babies and music everywhere! We were brought in to the tent which had been erected in the garden and were made the guests of honour. The people were thrilled to have us with them.

What we were not prepared for was the Belarussian 'moon-shine' called *samagong*. The wedding involved a whole series of toasts. Each small glass had to be raised and emptied in one gulp! The effects were indescribable, and if it had been a touch of radiation poisoning I had had the previous day, well, after the *samagong* it was well and truly exorcised out of my body! The lads joined in with the locals for some arm-wrestling (they were a poor match for the Belarussians!) and we 'girls' exhibited some Irish dancing, interspersed with plenty of 'yahoos'! Neither we nor the Belarussians will forget this wedding in a hurry!

10

Into the belly of the beast

[The No-Go Land]

It was like happening
   on the Marie Celeste,
entering a sometime home
   of a sometime town
with a table still
   laid for breakfast
and not a soul to be
   seen since the wind
blew all the arrows
   of the weathervanes
that way and invaders
   whisked everyone away.

Unmade beds hold
   the mould of
sleepers and a framed
   unknown woman cradles
a babushka-wrapped child
   and smiles into space.
An open book lies
   face down on a stand
waiting for a hand to
   turn it right side up
and children to be lulled
   again to never never land.
   Greg Delanty

Each day we drove closer to the exclusion zone. Finally the day came when we were to enter. We rose at 6 a.m. and breakfasted in our room. There was a rising tension but nobody spoke about it. We kept our conversation technical, about what needed to be done to ensure that the work was carried out with maximum speed and efficiency. None of us had any desire to hang around the Purple Zone.

In preparation we had agreed to take no risks. All four geiger counters were to be switched on permanently. We were to wear full protective clothing. We agreed that under no circumstances would any of us remove any of the clothing or masks.

We left at 6.30 a.m. to meet with the special police of the zone who would be accompanying us for the day. When we arrived at the fence of the 30-kilometre perimeter the guards awaited us. They introduced themselves as our 'hosts' to the zone. They told us that we must have luck on our side, as it had rained the previous night and therefore the threat from airborne radioactive particles was reduced. We felt suitably consoled!

We started to put on our protective clothing and the guards smiled and sniggered. These men were so macho that they boasted about never wearing any protective clothing or masks. They had looks of scorn particularly for the men in the crew. But we were determined not to be undermined by their foolishness and total disregard for their own personal safety. On the Ukrainian side of the exclusion zone everyone wore the clothing. The Belarussian guards seemed to be far too 'smart' for their own good. Most of these men lived just across the road from the 30-kilometre exclusion zone fence and all of them had young families. So they not only exposed themselves to huge amounts of radiation during their daily work, but they had the double exposure of also living in the zone.

I took our first geiger counter reading of the day and practically felt my heart stop with fright. It moved swiftly: 88 counts per minute . . . then 222, 411, 568, 634, 1,384, 1,800, 2,010! I was now registering levels that were 2,000 times greater than the internationally acceptable ones. This was not the end of the high readings, only the beginning. I gestured from behind my mask to tell the lads that we were already in very dangerous territory and to be very careful. Timing in the zone was of extreme importance and our filming had to be concluded within four hours. After that time, we had been advised, we would be putting ourselves in very serious danger. So regardless of whether we got the shots and sound, we would have to leave the 'Purple Zone' by 3 p.m. that afternoon. The pressure on the crew was enormous. The director, Gerry, knew the importance for the viewing audience of scenes from within the 30-kilometre zone, and the strain of the time pressure would make his job very difficult. He already knew that we would be limited in what could be filmed. His dilemma was what to prioritize and what to miss. He wanted to film everything, but it just wouldn't be physically possible.

We were split into two groups. Each was given two geiger counters. Dónal the cameraman was already having problems with the heat underneath his mask. It was making his concentration and focus very difficult. There would be times when he would have to risk taking down his mask in order to get his shots properly. The police took Ali, Dan, Gerry, Liam and Dónal in their jeep and they headed off in the direction of the Chernobyl reactor. Ali had to do her final 'piece to camera' in front of the burned-out reactor. Afterwards Ali told me about the silence and tension as they drove at break-neck speed along the dirt road to the reactor. The only thing that broke the silence was the sound of a Ukrainian military helicopter overhead. This was the start of a 'cat and mouse' game between the Belarussian police and the Ukrainian military. The jeep had entered the 'no man's land' area of the 'Purple Zone' which covers both sides of the border between the two countries. The helicopter was trying to chase the jeep out of the Ukrainian side of the border. The crew were quite alarmed about this development, as they knew that the military could have taken any action that took their fancy in response to the discovery of the jeep in their territory. The Belarussian guards were enjoying 'the game' and laughed as they finally managed to lose them in a wooded area. This incident added to the anxiety of the crew and to their resolve to get the pictures of the reactor with Ali in the foreground done in extra-quick time.

In the meantime Isobel and I stayed with the second police vehicle and our own van with the task of checking the houses around the deserted village we had parked in.

We proceeded to go deeper into the 'Purple Zone' areas, where the readings of the geiger counters were so enormous that several times they could not register the levels of radiation. The concentration in the air surpassed admissable levels sometimes by up to 4,000 times. It was a very strange and alien country – thousands of villages deserted, some burnt to the ground, submerged in concrete, others standing eerily in silence. A strange 'calm' descended on us as we slowly adjusted to what had to be done. Part of my function was to enter the deserted houses to see what remained of the people's lives.

As I stood in the middle of the road I couldn't decide which house to go into. As I half stumbled along the overgrown grassy verge outside a row of houses, I tried to make a decision. All sorts of questions ran around in my head. Which house would it be? The one with the lovely hand-made lace curtains? Or the house with the open front door? No, maybe it would be the house painted in my favourite colour, red. What about the house with the handsome glass porch full of overgrown geraniums?

I finally settled on a house with peeling blue paint, with a child's tricycle left propped up against the gate. As I opened the garden gate and walked to the front door I had an impulse to knock on the door or to cough out loud to let the people know there was someone outside – until I remembered that nobody lived there any more. I was faced with a padlocked door. I felt like a thief as I 'broke and entered' the first house by putting my boot to the door. Underneath my mask I became conscious of my own breathing sounds, which appeared to come from someone or something else. I was like an invader on a strange and alien planet. These thoughts rushed through my mind as I pushed in the broken front door, and a sense of unrest and uneasiness in the house surrounded me.

As I walked through this little place that once was full of life, I could almost fully imagine what it had been like on that fateful morning in 1986. People had been innocently sleeping in their beds or eating breakfast, when suddenly army tanks came rolling down their village streets, and men dressed in strange suits shouted to the people to get out of their beds, to leave their homes for ever. What must that have been like for the people? Chernobyl lurked over my shoulder and I shuddered. I felt immobilized by the wave of emotion that came over me. I wanted to cry but stopped myself.

Through the window of this house I caught a glimpse of a white-suited body coming towards me, and with great relief I signalled to say, 'I'm here, alone, waiting, waiting for human contact!'

I remember standing in someone's bedroom, looking at the imprint of the body that had lain in that bed on that fateful morning. I remember seeing a little table laid for the breakfast that had never been eaten. It lay before me, frozen in time for me to witness seven years later. I remember looking around and seeing photographs of the people whom this little house had protected – the grandparents, the parents, the children. An old Christmas card lay on the floor. A calendar hung on the wall, showing the date, 26th April 1986. The day the world changed for ever.

I felt very intrusive, voyeuristic even, as I went from house to house. I was the invader coming to see what the human species had done to themselves and their habitat.

We continued to walk through other deserted homes and came upon what had once been the village medical centre. Now all that was left was empty babies' cots and beds. Adjoining the medical centre we found what had once been a small library. Half burned books were all that remained. What had once been a source of pleasure and enlightenment had become a harbourer of danger, as the pages absorbed and held the invisible enemy of radiation.

I thought of the people who had lived in this village that we were now invading. All were peasant farming people who had been uprooted from their lives and land. Now they were rootless and useless in an alien urban environment where there was no need for their farming skills. They remained unemployed with no hope. The brokenness in their lives was immeasurable.

The Chernobyl accident has shown that damage to public health can be caused not only by radiation but also by a lack of integrity and honesty in those charged with protecting the public health interest. The Chernobyl disaster also shows us that we cannot measure or quantify the on-going and sometimes permanent psychological damage done to whole communities of people whose lives have been irrevocably changed.

I remember feelings of nausea as the film editor, Isobel, and I sat for hours waiting for the rest of the crew. I needed to vomit. My body was drenched with sweat underneath the dust suit and mask. On checking the geiger counter our driver became panicked, and he tried to drive out of the spot we were parked in. In his haste, the back wheels got stuck in the soft, dry earth. Isobel and I had to get out and push. As the wheels whirred, earth splashed into our faces – earth laden with radioactive particles. (What our driver had sensed was confirmed later when the new phenomenon of 'hot radioactive cocktails' was explained to us. These 'cocktails' are lethal mixes of strontium, caesium, plutonium and uranium.) Several minutes later we managed to get the van moving. We were both very shaken by what had happened. I felt intense fear inside the pit of my stomach. I wanted to cry, but I couldn't, as there was no way of wiping the tears from my face. The driver by this time was getting extremely agitated, as he had refused to wear any protective clothing, and he was now beginning to realize the foolishness of that refusal.

Looking around me, I found it so hard to comprehend that it would not be possible for people to live in these areas for thousands of years to come. Yet the exclusion zone had become home to a strange group called the 'bandits', who roamed around the area, living every day in a different deserted house. In one of the houses we visited we saw visible signs of someone hiding there – lumps of bread and a half-empty vodka bottle, as if someone had to leave in a hurry, perhaps when they heard the noise of our vehicle. Many of these people are war refugees from the far distant lands of Azerbaijan, finding refuge in the world's most radioactive environment.

But it was the deafening silence that eventually caused me the most disturbance. Silence . . . Silence . . . What was its meaning? Was it condemnation? Judgement? The ancient trees looked down upon us, as if watching, waiting for the answer to their question, 'Why? What has humanity done?' I answered, 'We have lost our way.' I was reminded of a line from Hindu scripture: 'Now I am become death, destroyer of worlds.'

This sobering communication with nature was broken by the sound of the returning jeep, with the rest of the crew. Everyone was visibly shaken. They had been chased by a Ukrainian military helicopter which had tried to prevent the crew from filming too close to the reactor.

The time had come for us to leave this strange place, not with much regret but with great sadness. When we reached the guards' hut at the entrance to the zone we removed our protective suits with great care. We took photographs standing by the exclusion zone sign. Then we got back in the van and finally left this madness behind. Our silence and emotional exhaustion filled the van. We were each affected by what had happened and we expressed it in different ways. What had sustained us through this nightmare had been the power and strength of the friendship and respect that had grown between us.

That night was our last in Khoniki. Strangely enough, we were sad to leave the place. None of us could verbalize why it was exactly. I felt as if I had survived several lifetimes and was happy to be left alive. We had by now bonded together as a very close team. While working in the zone it was as if no other life existed for us. We were suspended in time and place. Leaving Khoniki was painful. Coming home was equally painful, like 're-entry' from another planet. In many ways it was. None of us would ever be quite the same.

Coming back to Ireland was full of mixed emotions for all of us. Of course, we were all delighted to return safely, but we were thinking of those we had left behind, and the severity of their situation took its personal and emotional toll on all of us. Our resolve, however, to make a powerful witness of the Chernobyl story was stronger than ever.

Isobel the editor and Gerry the director now worked for three months in front of editing machines, trying to make sense of what we had recorded and filmed. The end result was something very special. The documentary was finished by October 1993 and was given its World Premiere in Dublin at the Irish Film Centre, launched by the Minister for Arts, Culture and the Gaeltacht, Michael D. Higgins.

The night of the Premiere was very exciting. The crew were all assembled, along with friends and family. Each of us was wondering anxiously what this very special invited audience would think of our work. There were many celebrities present at the launch, including Ali's husband Bono and fellow members of the

Above: The 'entombed' Chernobyl reactor. (Courtesy of Anatoly Kleschuk)

Left: The Dreamchaser film crew. Clockwise from left: Gerry Hoban, Dan Birch, Donal Gilligan, Ali Hewson, myself and Liam Cabot. (Courtesy of Conor Horgan and *Image* magazine)

Right: 'Small Igor' during the filming of *Black Wind, White Land* in 1993 at the Children's Number One Home for abandoned children. (Adi Roche)

Below: Igor Shik, a former laundry worker and 'liquidator' showing his reward from the Government, a card calling him a 'good patriot'. All compensation for the liquidators was cancelled in September 1995. (Courtesy of Donal Gilligan)

Right: An old peasant farmer from the 'purple zone' trying to sell her pig at the food market in Khoniki. (Courtesy of Donal Gilligan)

Below: A scene in a shop. Note the 'old computer', the abacus, still used extensively in Belarus. (Courtesy of Donal Gilligan)

Left: A woman fetching water in the deserted town of Bragin. (Courtesy of Donal Gilligan)

Below: The Dreamchaser film crew working in the 'purple zone', just 10km from the burnt-out reactor. (Courtesy of film editor Isobel Stephenson)

Above: The old woman who reminded me so much of my grandmother, with her son, during the filming of the 'Day of the Dead' in Lipa. (Adi Roche)

КОНОВАЛОВ
АНАТОЛИЙ
ВЛАДИМИРОВИЧ
19${}^{11}_{08}$63-19${}^{13}_{08}$88

The old man who made
us scrambled eggs
washed down with vodka
in the semi-deserted
village of Mikulichi. (Adi
Roche)

The village graveyard that overlooks Lipa is full of gravestones of deaths recorded in 1988. Villagers claim this young man was the victim of radiation. (Courtesy of Donal Gilligan)

The first convoy of ambulances to leave Ireland in September 1994, shown here with mechanics and crew.

Above: A very special moment for two small girls, Alla and Lydia, as they are greeted by the President of Ireland. Alla's parents committed suicide, unable to cope with the tragedy of Chernobyl. Lydia was conceived in the 'purple zone' and suffers from stunted growth. (Courtesy of Peter Casey)

Below: With HRH, the Duchess of York and Ali Hewson at our first meeting.

A contaminated house in the main street of the now deserted village of Lipa. It is in the process of being dismantled, one of many to be sold and transplanted to the Ukraine as holiday homes. (Courtesy of Donal Gilligan)

Sad reminders of times gone by scattered on the floor in Lipa. (Courtesy of Donal Gilligan)

Below: With the Smolsky family and friend Pavel in December 1994. Within an hour of my arrival at the house, they were evacuated forever from Strelichevi. (Courtesy of Donal Gilligan)

The main street in Strelichevi. The cart is about to be loaded for evacuation. (Courtesy of Donal Gilligan)

Right: The man from Azerbaijan who guards one of the radiation zone entrances into the village of Tulgovichi. (Courtesy of Donal Gilligan)

Below: 'Dr Zhivago', the 'husband' who awaited me in exchange for two horses and a cart. (Courtesy of Donal Gilligan)

A loving moment in the Children's Number One
Home. (Courtesy of Donal Gilligan)

Linda Walker and I enjoy giving a helping hand in the
Children's Number One Home. (Courtesy of Donal Gilligan)

Some of the Downs
Syndrome children
abandoned at the
Children's Number One
Home. (Courtesy of
Donal Gilligan)

A Physical Education class for the orphans at
Volozhin orphanage, situated in a 'hot spot' area
outside Minsk. (Courtesy of Donal Gilligan)

With Nicolei and Lyuda in the Soligorsk
orphanage. (Courtesy of Linda Walker)

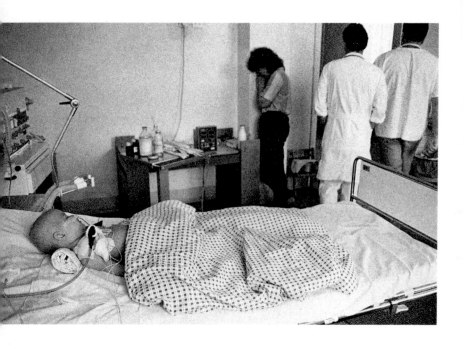

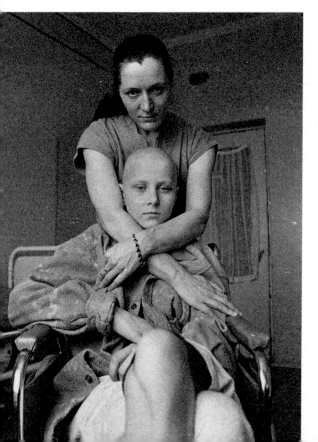

A mother grieving the final moments of her daughter's life, at the Oncology Institute in Minsk. (Courtesy of Anatoly Kleschuk)

A tender moment for Natasha and her mother. Natasha is alive because of a life-saving operation in Germany. On her first visit to Ireland in 1995 she won the hearts of the Kinsale people. They have 'adopted' her and regularly bring her back for treatment. (Courtesy of Anatoly Kreschuk)

Back in Gomel, in April 1995, Sasha and Vitaly have much to smile about on the road to recovery after their life-saving operations. (Courtesy of Donal Gilligan)

The Russian Orthodox Christmas Day is 6 January, and Evgenia wakes up to find a new friend sitting on the bed. (Courtesy of Billy MacGill)

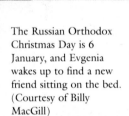

Paul Newman and I sharing a laugh at the opening of the Barretstown Gang Camp, Kildare, Ireland, in July 1995. (Courtesy of Brendan Hughes)

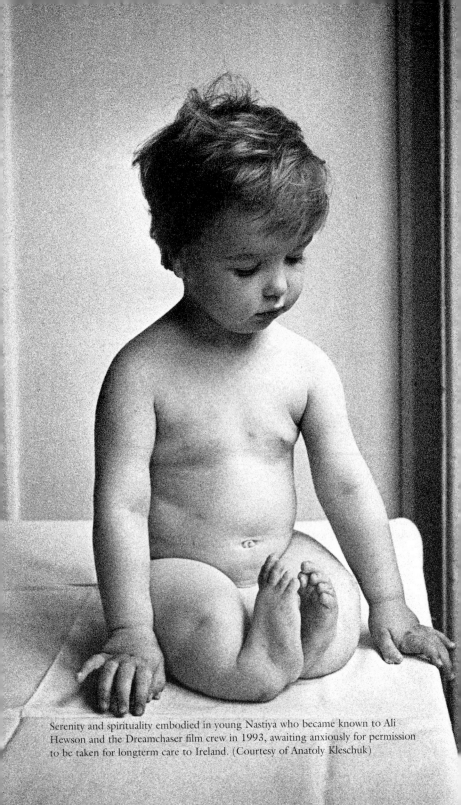

Serenity and spirituality embodied in young Nastiya who became known to Ali Hewson and the Dreamchaser film crew in 1993, awaiting anxiously for permission to be taken for longterm care to Ireland. (Courtesy of Anatoly Kleschuk)

band U2, who have consistently supported the work of CND and Greenpeace. Ned O'Hanlon, Executive Producer of the documentary, introduced the programme with quiet enthusiasm, and left the rest to the audience. 'Black Wind – White Land, Living with Chernobyl', rolled up on the screen and the house lights dimmed.

The next hour was agony. Sitting through the programme and watching all the familiar faces and places brought up the entire experience again. I felt tears well up in my eyes, but was afraid that this was more because I personally knew every frame of this programme. I worried that it wouldn't mean the same thing to the audience, who had no personal connection with anything or anyone on the screen. The Belarussian music, written specially by a young musician who was a survivor from the zones, swept the audience along, adding an appropriate depth of feeling. Finally the credits rolled. Silence from the audience. Then came the burst of applause. The audience gave it the 'seal of approval' by giving a standing ovation to the crew.

The reviews that followed were wonderful. Complete support and sympathy was the order of the day. Interview after interview followed. The screening on national Irish television the following night got the highest TAM rating of the year. The entire country stopped and watched. This was just the start of what would follow over the coming months. The documentary was shown five times on the Discovery satellite network. It was shown also in such countries as Japan, New Zealand, Switzerland, the Netherlands, Germany, Hungary, Poland, Slovenia, the Czech Republic, South Africa and Malaysia. By the end of 1994 it had received many awards, including one at the Intercom '94 Awards, and first prize at the Golden Gate Awards in San Francisco, USA.

So what had started out as just a dream in my head had finally become reality. The truth was finally known to the world.

11

The medical effects of Chernobyl

The Belarussian Necklace

Four young frightened girls
Waiting for their turn
Will it hurt? Will I survive?
The lessons quickly learned
They lie there in their beds of fear
It could be you or me, but they must pay the price
For man's inhumanity.

Four young frightened girls
Want to live their lives
Want to find a sweetheart
Want to be young wives.
They want safety for their children
In a land that's free from fear
They want love and life and laughter
And a future they can face
With their children's necks unblemished
Not a Belarussian red necklace.

   Mags Whiting

Petr Kravchanka, the Foreign Minister of Belarus, has commented, '*The whole future of our nation is in jeopardy. The Chernobyl disaster was like a nuclear attack on our republic in peacetime, and we are only just beginning to see the consequences of the tragedy.*'

   With that chilling statement ringing in my head, I try to make sense of something that there is little sense to. How can I convey this tragedy in words? The scale of what has happened to a whole race of people and their land is almost beyond comprehension. The way I know best is to present the stark consequences as they have been given to me. Sometimes I wake up sweating, thinking that I've dreamed it all up, that it cannot be true. In seconds the ugly reality seeps into my mind and I know that the nightmare is real. We are witnessing the slow death of a people.

The radiation reached the general public externally when they were exposed to radioactivity in the cloud or through radioactive elements deposited in the soil. The internal exposure occurred through inhalation of the 'dust' from the cloud or ingestion via contaminated food. It is the internal radiation that causes the most danger.

It is difficult to assess the total damage, because the medical records of over 670,000 Belarussians registered with Chernobyl-related problems mysteriously disappeared from a major hospital in Minsk. This 'theft' included the vital data from 20,000 resettlements in the severely contaminated regions of Mogilev and Gomel. What is know is that in the three affected countries – Russia, Belarus and Ukraine – over 1.3 million people are registered with Chernobyl-linked health problems. Many people believe this figure to be a serious underestimation of the true numbers. At a UNESCO Conference on Chernobyl in 1994 it was revealed that between 3 and 4 million children in the three countries are now estimated to be affected. Health deterioration includes respiratory problems, nosebleeds, vomiting, severe headaches and depression.

What has further concealed the true extent of the aftermath is yet another secret decree which was passed in 1988 in Moscow, banning doctors from naming radiation as the cause of illness or death. Bearing in mind this control over information, I salute the courage of those medical personnel who have risked revealing the truth. By talking to me and the crew, they risked much of their own personal safety and professional future, and yet they chose to do so in order that the true story could be revealed to the world.

The long-term effects of Chernobyl are chilling in the extreme. According to Professor John Gofman (Professor Emeritus of molecular and cell biology, University of Berkeley, California), there will be 475,000 fatal cancer deaths and an equal number of non-fatal cancers worldwide. Hearing such figures, I am reminded of the universality of radiation. It is an invisible death that knows no territorial boundaries; it is ruthless in its path of destruction; it is carried to the four corners of the planet. We have all become victims and survivors of Chernobyl.

The most significant short-term contaminant isotopes are the iodine ones, and in particular, Iodine 131, which has a half-life of eight days. It is either inhaled as a dust particle or ingested in cow's milk. Once it finds its way into the human body it is mainly absorbed by the thyroid. Since infants and children have more active thyroids and also drink a lot more milk than adults, they become the high-risk category group.

In 1993, I spoke to Dr Evgeni Demidchik, Director of the Thyroid Tumour Clinic in Minsk. His special concern is the thyroid damage among children. For eight days after the accident Iodine 131 was breathed and consumed in food by the whole Belarussian population. The children received a dose in excess of 1,000 Rad to their thyroid glands. The permissible level is 30, and even this is considered by many to be too much. You could say that the people were attacked by radioactive iodine. In northern Belarus, 250 miles away from Chernobyl, the concentration in the air surpassed admissible levels by 1,000 times. Over the next 15–20 years it is estimated that over 40,000 children in Belarus alone with contract cancer of the thyroid. Of these 10,000 will be malignancies; 1,000 children will die.

Dr Demidchik has conducted the most comprehensive study of the development of thyroid tumours in Belarus, a study that began in 1966, when thyroid cancer was a rare disease. After the Chernobyl disaster, he began to see a marked increase in cancer of the thyroid in children. In the two decades before Chernobyl, there was less than one case per year. From the time of the disaster up to 1995, 379 children received surgery for thyroid cancer. All these new cases came from the most contaminated regions: 30% came from the town of Pinsk in the eastern part of Brest province, and over 60% came from the affected parts of Gomel. Pinsk was seriously contaminated by radioactive iodine in the days after the disaster. All the children surveyed were born shortly before or during the time of the disaster. According to Dr Demidchik, because the native diet was already seriously lacking in natural iodine, the people's thyroid glands absorbed the radioactive iodine 'like sponges', because the body was unable to determine the difference between radioactive and natural iodine. Where potassium iodine tablets were promptly distributed to children – for example, in Mogilev, a heavily contaminated area – the impact was far less severe. The number of cancers was less because the local health officials had issued the iodine tablets in time.

The tumour must be discovered and removed at an early stage. The Belarussian procedure involves the removal of only the affected area and not the entire gland. Removal of the entire gland is the common practice in the West. Demidchik says that thyroid tumours are very aggressive and the cancer spreads rapidly to other parts of the body. Thus early diagnosis is imperative if the children's lives are to be saved.

The incidence of this disorder has considerably exceeded the average world level and its rate of increase is surpassing all the predictions of the world's experts. In Belarus alone there has been a 24-fold increase in cancer of the thyroid gland; in the Gomel region there is a 100-fold increase.

One of the appalling things I heard from many different doctors was the lack of willingness in the West to publish a lot of the material researched jointly by Belarussian and Western scientists about the effects on the thyroid gland. Perhaps one of the reasons for the lack of co-operation in sharing this vital information with the world could be that Iodine 131, which is known to be the principal thyroid-seeking fallout isotope, is discharged by the nuclear industry in the West. It is also the abundant isotope found following nuclear weapons tests, and the American government is constantly being petitioned for compensation by cancer survivors who live or have lived near the Nevada nuclear weapons test site.

In March 1995 the World Health Organisation finally helped to break the international silence on damage to the thyroid gland by issuing the results of findings by WHO and scientists from Belarus, the Ukraine and Russia on increases in childhood thyroid cancer. These findings, the results of a pilot project on thyroid disease in which 70,000 children were screened, finally give credence to the mammoth pioneering work of Dr Demidchik and his team. A clear link has now been established between the regions contaminated by radiation from the accident and the increase in childhood thyroid cancer. Importantly, the thyroid cancers are the indicators of other diseases, such as breast cancer, that are very likely to follow. Unfortunately, the further expansion of such vital projects is dependent on funding, which is not particularly forthcoming.

During our filming in Belarus we visited some of the thyroid cancer children. They all had the tell-tale bandage across their necks. When it would be removed, they would have the permanent looped scar from ear to ear, the 'Belarussian necklace', marking them for ever as Chernobyl victims. In cramped hospital rooms, the children shyly told us about missing their family and friends. Children who had had their thyroid glands removed were in the same room as children awaiting the operation. They were made very anxious by seeing the dreadful suffering of the others. Many of them were unwilling to talk. They just languished in bed with dispirited expressions. Ali talked to Helena, who was about to have her thyroid removed the following day. Helena was 16 and was terrified of the operation. We promised to visit her after the operation. When we returned, we were very upset by the severity of what she had suffered. She was very weak and unable to talk. The crew left her gifts and told her how brave and beautiful she was. She cried. We left.

We visited other hospitals and talked to many doctors, who told us there had been a marked increase in other health effects, including disorders involving the endocrine system. It was revealed at the second International Congress (Minsk, 1993) that the incidence of goitre disorders had increased by a factor of 40. The incidence of diabetes mellitus was now 163.8 per 100,000 people, as compared to 51.0 per 100,000 before the disaster. Blood disorders and disorders of the blood-producing organs had increased by 9.4 times, mainly in the form of anaemia. There was a considerable growth of neurocirculatory dystonia (problems with the nerves controlling the circulation) and of different cataracta (an eleven-fold increase in five years!).

An increase in cases of bone, bladder and kidney cancer and cases of lymphoreticulosarcoma has been registered in the Gomel region. Another problem that was not predicted relates to the damage to the immune system. These illnesses, caused by Chernobyl, are referred to as 'Chernobyl AIDS' and are caused by the effects of strontium, which is accepted by the body because it has a close resemblance to calcium. It gets absorbed by the bone structure of the body and remains there for a very long time. Strontium is highly radioactive and has a disastrous effect on bone marrow and bone growth in children during their growing period. It takes anything up to three years before the damage caused by strontium becomes visible. The weakening of the immune system that it causes can probably explain the rising number of cancer cases. Many doctors have expressed a deep concern about the current increases in cancers, and about the cancers which are already present but not yet evident. These cancers are now able to break through because the body's immunity against cancer cells has been very seriously undermined and damaged.

Many doctors are not so concerned about the gamma radiation that passes through the human body (though that kind of radiation is still too high in some areas) as they are about the lethal radioactive particles of caesium, plutonium and strontium in the topsoil and roadside dust, ready to be stirred up, inhaled or eaten in contaminated food.

The health deterioration in Belarus in the post-disaster period is characterized by a persistent growth in the morbidity rate among children, especially of younger ages, as well as among pregnant women and women of child-bearing age. It is also characterized by an increase in birth disorders and a growth in infant mortality. In the radiation zones the birth rates have dropped by 50%. For the first time in Belarussian history, the death rate is higher than the birth rate.

We found that privately people would speak about thousands of women who wanted abortions because of foetal damage from radiation. According to the American Dr Robert Gale (who performed bone marrow transplants on some of the Chernobyl victims), about 100,000 abortions have been carried out in the three affected regions, abortions purely related to radiation. There is no 'choice' involved. The power of the so-called 'peaceful' atom has taken away the power of women's right to make their own decisions. As a result, many of the women feel disempowered and angry. Belarussian women are just like women the world over. They love their children and cherish the joy of giving birth. The birth experience is all too frequently turned into sadness, and many women who find they have given birth to children that are ill or deformed leave their hospital beds, walk out, leaving their babies behind. Chernobyl is changing their joy into never-ending sorrow.

The Belarussian government is implementing a system of medicogenetic assistance to the population. In 1992 a medico-genetic centre was opened in Gomel. There are plans to introduce similar centres in Mogilev, Vitebsk and Grodno. As a result of this programme, 403 abortions were carried out in 1993, owing to irreversible foetal pathologies. When the National Programme is fully implemented, it will prevent the birth of over 1,000 children per year with incurable diseases. The number of gestations with foetal developmental defects identified by limited ultrasound scanning increased from 2.30 per 1,000 pregnancies in 1991 to 4.04 per 1,000 in 1993.

The main long-term concern is the effect of continued, rela-tively low-dose exposure to radioactivity. We are looking only at ten years after the accident. What does the future hold? One of the doctors told us that the Belarussian race is threatened with extinction because their gene pool (their children) is now 'unclean'. Even the term 'unclean' is one that I resent; it is a dreadful indictment of today's world. The appearance of a whole range of cancers, neo-natal deaths, low weight births (500 grams) and short pregnancies (now seven months) are all part of the legacy of Chernobyl. Because the hospitals have very few incuba-tors, the chances of the babies surviving is greatly reduced. The children are dying, their water, land and air are poisoned, but Chernobyl is still shrouded in secrecy.

Many doctors we spoke to verified that there has been a 250% increase in congenital birth deformities and a 100% increase in childhood cancer and leukaemia. Doctors in Belarus maintain that their success in curing childhood leukaemias can be as low as 10–15% because of the lack of medicines. In the West we can cure up to 85% of all children suffering from cancer.

In one of the hospitals we visited in Soligorsk, a doctor told us about having to burn the bodies of 22 babies, most of whom had been born with no organs, to try to establish how much radiation they had absorbed in the womb. The same doctor spoke about other babies born with fully blown leukaemia.

The chief doctor in one of Gomel's leading hospitals told us that 90% of Belarussian children living in the zones are unhealthy now. He genuinely fears for the future of the Belarussian race. He asked me, 'How would you feel if your race of people were threatened with extinction?' I could not answer. I began to understand what lay behind his question and I was challenged by its implications. Emotionally, psychologically, is it possible to live with such a fear and threat? Radiation does not affect us only in a physical way. It is not a true picture just to consider the health effects without including the social, psychological and moral consequences of the impact of radiation: the destruction of a society's structural organization, people's real fears for their children, the helplessness that emerges. The intangibility of the 'enemy' makes coping with it far less real or possible. Eventually a state of inertia sets in; people become immobilized and just give up. People's powerless state is reflected in the 1,000% increase in suicide in the zones.

The authorities try to dismiss people's fears and emotions by labelling it 'radiophobia'. Nice and simple! Blame the victims! The nuclear promoters of this world have never taken cognizance of the interconnectedness of the physical and psychological trauma caused by nuclear disasters. They have packaged the 'effects' of a nuclear war or accident into nice neat sums and equations on their computers. Nowhere in any of their computer calculations have they considered the genuine fears of human beings. In Belarus there is widespread uneasiness among people, a constant fear of being exposed to radiation, and an awareness of the permanence of the threat to their health and lives has taken a severe toll. It must not be dismissed.

There now exists a real threat to the gene pool of Belarus. The potential genetic threat to the population in the next few years or decades may result, particularly in the sphere of marriage and other human relations, in the emergence of a band of 'outcasts'. This happened after the bombing of Hiroshima and Nagasaki, when the survivors became known as *Hibashuka*. Many of them experienced discrimination and still feel like outcasts even to this day in Japan. Nobody wanted to marry them, employ them or be friends with them, for fear of contamination and because of ignorance. Many of them committed suicide, as they were unable to cope with the isolation and rejection: a parallel picture of the Chernobyl survivors. Time and time again people from all walks of life expressed their deep sense of being stigmatized and 'branded'. This phenomenon has left many people's confidence and self-esteem in tatters. The psyche of the nation, either consciously or unconsciously, is left confused and damaged.

A quietly spoken doctor in the Gomel region told me about the difficulties for the medical profession in revealing the truth about the accident, since a secret decree had been made in May 1991 forbidding doctors to cite radiation as the cause of illness or death. The official who passed the decree is a man called Shcherbina. The same man ordered the replacement town for the town of Chernobyl to be built in an area that was as radioactive as the original town.

In a different children's hospital in Gomel, another doctor painted an all too familiar bleak medical picture: the constant growth of blood diseases such as leukaemia, haemophilia and lymphoma. She showed us a graph of the cancer increase since 1986. The graph was shocking, but Dr Oxana pointed out that this was not a true reflection of the situation, because many of the children never even reached the hospital for medical attention.

One of the doctors answered my question about his thoughts on the future of the Belarussian people by posing yet another question: 'What happens when sick children become sick adults and have even sicker children?' The gene pool of the race is under such severe pressure that over decades the cumulative effects will take a very heavy toll.

During our time at this hospital we were joined by a Gomel television crew and by parents of children in the cancer ward. We listened to the mothers, who made a very special plea for the lives of their children.

We were told that sometimes the children died because they came from rural areas and were diagnosed too late. The mothers told us how they often had to carry their children great distances to get to the hospital because they had no cars and public transport was very limited and unreliable. The mothers and doctors cried. It was hard not to be moved by the tragedy of their situation. But amidst their pain there was also great strength. These women, encouraged by the doctors, had started to organize themselves and look for justice for their children. This was the first group we had come across in Belarus whom we felt had managed to cross over from despair to empowerment, and had recognized their abilities to seek their basic human right to protect the lives of their children.

At some point during the meeting Dónal, our cameraman, whispered to me to offer them an ambulance as a gesture of help. The response to our offer was perplexing. Instead of 'Oh yes, thank you very much', we got what appeared to be a muddled debate among our hosts. We were not expecting such a response! When it was finally translated we learned they had always dreamed of having an ambulance for the children, but in their wildest imagination they had never thought it would happen! Then along came an offer of an ambulance slipped into the middle of a conversation about the children's health. They were unable to respond with a basic 'yes' because they were overwhelmed! Their dream had come true at last.

Later, as we walked the wards, meeting and greeting the children for the first time, I wasn't full of sadness but was filled with a sense that just maybe we could save the lives of some of the children of these brave mothers. In one of the wards there was a lone 14-year-old girl with beautiful, long, blonde hair loosely tied with a red bow. The doctor whispered that they had just diagnosed her illness as leukaemia. We were the first to know, even before her mother. What lay ahead for this young girl? No one could say.

As we passed through ward after ward, we met many more mothers and heard about how they had to share the tiny beds with their children. When a child was admitted to the hospital, the mother would normally come to stay until the child recovered. This had put enormous pressure on the families' already strained finances. Many of the mothers had to leave their jobs and had no guarantee that they would be re-employed later. So the 'hidden' effects of Chernobyl must include the economic burden upon the suffering families. For many of the families, the mother is the sole bread-winner, so when illness strikes a child, it not only affects the family emotionally but economically as well. They receive $2.50 per month in state support.

The mothers have had a tremendously strong faith in God. 'We are grateful for every day we have with our children,' they said. 'Each day our children survive is a precious gift from God.' The courage of these women and doctors left a marked impression on us.

They said they sometimes saw convoys of aid passing by the gates of the hospital, but few stopped and entered. We resolved that one day soon a special medical aid truck along with an ambulance would arrive at their hospital.

As we left the hospital one of the mothers gave us a special letter and asked that it be shown to everyone so that people might respond and help to save the lives of their dying children. The letter speaks for itself. Here it is:

People of good will, help our children. With pain and hope we apply to you. We are mothers of sick children from Gomel region. The common Chernobyl misfortune united all of us into one organization, 'Children Haemotology' by name. There are children in our organization who suffer from heavy blood diseases: leukaemia, lymphoma, haemophilia and others.

They need help.

We, the parents and doctors of the haemotology department of the Gomel region hospital, fight for the lives of our children. Sometimes we have a success, sometimes not. It is a pity to say, but sometimes all our efforts end badly. The situation is very serious. There is not enough medicine to help all our sick children. And the children die . . .

Many of the parents have left work to give all their time and all their efforts to these children. But we have no opportunities to take care of children-invalids who became sick after the Chernobyl catastrophe.

We need medicine, vitamins, ecologically pure products. The children need to improve their health outside of our sick country. Our organization was founded not long ago, and we have no connections with foreign charity organizations. We need addresses of people who can help our children to improve their health.

That is why we apply to all people of good will. Sick children wait for your help and in the hearts of mothers there can be a hope for the future. We shall be thankful for every support. We believe that kindness will save the world.

In the midst of such emotion it is hard to write about the lighter side of our work in Belarus. But believe you me, there was always a lighter side, and our jokes and laughter became something we relied on increasingly as we became more affected ourselves by the lives and situation of the people. For instance, in the middle of filming at one hospital Dónal the cameraman told Gerry and Liam that he has had a camera jam. None of them seemed to be particularly worried, as we were in the middle of a city and assumed that such a minor problem could be solved quite easily. Not so! Much to our amazement, this 'slight' problem became a major one, as we were unable to find any place that had the right tool to release the jam. We spent hours going from jeweller to jeweller in the hope that one of them would be able to help. If we were unable to release the jam – well, it would have meant no more filming.

As we were waiting for Dónal and Gerry outside yet another jeweller, the rest of us turned our gloom and anxiety into a highly entertaining period. Dan, our sound engineer, always the easygoing fun guy, came up trumps yet again to lift even the most downcast of us. He popped out of the van, put the ghetto blaster on the side of the road and to the sounds of the group Crowded House danced in a John Travolta fashion, using a lamp-post as his partner! Well, you should have seen the reaction of the passers-by! They had never seen anything like it! When the others returned from the jeweller's, they hadn't solved the problem, but at least we were all in better spirit!

Eventually, the following day, three towns later, we found a jeweller who was willing to risk the job. The camera was fixed and we all started to relax in the knowledge that the documentary could continue to be made – and, of course, Dan could stop dancing, until the next problem arose! He provided the tonic for all of us when things went wrong. By this time each of our very different personalities was emerging, which was an interesting developmental stage for all of us. What could easily have been a recipe for disaster in human relations and therefore in our work luckily proved every day to be a strengthening friendship between all of us.

Many radioactive elements appear to have the same composition as the natural and vital minerals that our bodies need. For example:

Plutonium is the most toxic substance man has ever produced, and it does not exist in nature. The body treats it as iron, due to its chemical similarity. It gets distributed by the blood system to feed growing cells. It therefore can cause a variety of cancers and blood disorders.

Caesium 137 is mistaken by the body as potassium, which is needed by every living cell. It then concentrates in the muscles.

Iodine 131 is absorbed by the thyroid gland, which cannot determine whether it is natural or radioactive iodine. The thyroid gland controls all growth. Iodine 131 causes thyroid disorders and cancer of the thyroid.

Strontium 90: the body is fooled into accepting this element as calcium. It gets distributed throughout the bone structure of the body and can cause any number of cancers or leukaemias, along with numerous other health problems.

Penetrating Power of Different Types of Radiation

Alpha
Beta
X-ray (medical)
Gamma ray
Neutrons

Human Hand — Aluminium — Thin Lead — Thicker Lead — Concrete

12

Death of the land

Radiation

The photo could be of a cornfield anywhere,
but for the two forlorn, elderly gentlemen
with Tolstoy beards standing in the foreground.

The taller one to the right holds out
a loaf of bread on white linen
embroidered with a crewel flower that's upside

down and hung over his unseen hands.
The man on the left is hardly taller than
what appears to be a bumper crop.

He holds a makeshift banner that could belong
to any hippie demo declaring MAKE LOVE
NOT WAR or LIVE AND LET LIVE, but I can't

decipher the black banner's Belarussian.
The white letters look jumbled and words back
to front, reminding me of what 'live' becomes

when spelt backwards and what's hidden
behind everything these men live for now,
caught in a cornfield that could be anywhere.
   Greg Delanty

Not only has radiation endangered the genetic future of those
exposed to it, but its evil power of destruction has also damaged
the intricate cycle of all life. The suffering is medical, environmental, emotional, psychological and economical. The greatest
resource of every country is its land, and great damage has been

inflicted on the natural resources, water management systems and agriculture, of Belarus.

A total of 480,000 hectares of farming land, including 230,000 hectares of arable land, have been withdrawn from agricultural production. The territory adjacent to the River Prypyat, which had been a major meat and dairy producing area, has been turned into a depopulated radiation zone. The River Prypyat is highly radioactive, and since it feeds into the River Dnieper in the Ukraine, it has caused the silt bed of the Dnieper to become radioactive. The Dnieper is now the world's most radioactive river.

As Belarus has lost practically a quarter of its most fertile agricultural land, one of the most serious problems is soil clean-up and decontamination. The tried and tested ways of dealing with this problem – deep reploughing, removal of the contaminated soil level, clean earth backfilling and soil isolation – are either impossible, ineffective or economically unfeasible in Belarus. Experiments in decontamination have had frightening effects already. In the town of Bragin the people and the land were subjected to massive 'chemical cocktails' sprayed upon them from aircraft in a so-called effort to reduce the radiation levels. This did reduce the radiation levels, but the price paid was a high one. The land that was sprayed is now dead – all its nutrients have been killed off. The residents are falling ill. In advance of the experiment the government took the precaution of evacuating the men with skills, but it left the women, children and old people.

The radioactive contamination of the land is not the only danger posed. The use of chemicals in the attempts to reduce the radiation has had effects on the natural ecological balance. Large environmental problems that had already existed were now aggravated by an increase of nitrates and other chemicals in the soil.

There is simply not enough uncontaminated farmland left to feed the population. The spraying that took place to try to reduce the radionuclides in vegetables and fruit has had an alarming effect. The quantity of micro-elements in the crops has also sharply decreased. So the quality and nutritional value of the food are very reduced while the radionuclides remain. The scientific agencies left with the task of monitoring both the food and the land are astonishingly ill-equipped and, due to lack of transport, manage to monitor only 30% of the land and food. Thus the millions of people living on the other 70% of the land have to guess whether their food or land is radioactive or not.

Decontamination is not producing the results hoped for, as the radioactivity is spreading at a frightening rate throughout the country and beyond. Radioactive substances from the Chernobyl accident are spreading out in to the environment much more quickly than expected. According to the Russian geological chemist, Waleri Kopejkin, even the Ukrainian capital Kiev is under threat: 'If the Ukraine would implement the international accepted standards for Strontium 90, we would have to evacuate Kiev.'

Experts are in a quandary now as to what to do about the land. They have three options: (1) to abandon all efforts and to wait for the radioisotopes to decay, or for the upper soil layers to experience some self-purification; (2) to extract the radionuclides from the soil; (3) to expedite the migration of radionuclides in the soil.

The first possibility is already being done within the exclusion zone. The second and third options still require enormous scientific study. The main problem with option (2) would be the extremely large quantities of waste that would be generated; the difficulty, therefore, of treating the secondary waste makes this a highly unlikely alternative. The final option has possibly the most chance of success but is fraught with difficulties, as there would be the risk that the radionuclides would combine with elements in the upper soil layers, thereby slowing down the natural process of migration. If this method were to be considered seriously, it would entail researching into the properties and behaviours of strontium, americium, caesium and plutonium in various soils regarding their absorption qualities with different soil components and the kinetics of the isotope exchanges of these radioelements. To date, there is still insufficient information to implement this option.

The opinions of scientists both in Belarus and abroad differ as to the admissible levels of radioactive contamination in food and fodder. Attempts are being made to restore the soil and reduce the radiation levels in crops and animals, but these are proving to be quite unsuccessful. There has been no substantial reduction in the radioactivity in the soil and therefore in the products. Dairy farming, sheep-rearing and the cultivation of buckwheat, flax, legumes and other crops have been discontinued totally in some areas. Huge quantities of chemicals have been used to try to clean the soil, but this has caused severe damage to the natural vitamins in vegetables and fruit. For instance, the level of vitamin C content is now zero, and there is a sharp decrease in the quantity of micro-elements. Thus the quality of food products has been reduced, while unfortunately the radioactivity has not been reduced. Multivitamins are therefore badly needed.

It has become impossible for farmers to know if their land and its produce are 'clean' or not. Some areas will be radioactive for 24,000 years, which is the half-life of the highly radioactive material plutonium. A millionth of a gram of plutonium is enough to cause lung cancer.

Because of the severe economic situation of Belarus, the government is unable to supply its population with imported 'clean' food, and therefore the people have to eat the food produced by their own farmers. People have no choice other than to eat radioactive food. The main sources of contamination are therefore the food-chain and the water system. The accident has already cost eight annual budgets – 100 billion roubles. Near-crisis trends in the economy hinder the emergency measures that need to be implemented.

Five of the six regions of Belarus are contaminated, but the farmers are forced to continue agricultural production because there is nowhere left with non-contaminated farmland to provide the population with adequate 'clean' food supplies. Within the contaminated zones there are 3,678 inhabited towns and villages, most of which will never be evacuated.

There are on-going major problems, according to many experts, for those living in the zones, because there is a constant danger of secondary contamination of the soil by airborn radio-nuclides which occur in dust storms, brush/bush fires in forests and on peat beds, adding further radioactive movement. The final secondary contamination is from water erosion. This in effect recontaminates an already contaminated area with further amounts of such radioactive elements as Strontium 90 and Casesium 137. The most dangerous time of year for such occurrences is during the dry, hot summers experienced in Belarus.

These problems lead to the spreading of chronic diseases in

cattle and bacterial infections in young animals, which eventually affect the food chain. The constant difficulty this provides for the production of clean milk, for example, means that a complex process of cattle rearing is required. Most of the contaminated milk and vegetables are produced by private farms, which are subject to spot-checks for radionuclides. Unfortunately the spot-checks are by no means sufficient to control the amount of radioactive food that ends up on the stalls of towns and villages, to be bought and consumed by the local community.

The exclusion zones are now fast becoming giant experimental laboratories for all kinds of researchers from the West, who are paying much-needed hard currency to come and live and work in this bizarre radioactive land. We were told by local people in the Khoniki area that scientists were busy propagating seeds from irradiated trees and feeding various animals with contaminated fish from the rivers and streams, and then watching and waiting for possible mutations. They were also breeding calves from cows which had remained on the contaminated land since the accident.

It is just a catalogue of horrors. The land crisis is further exacerbated by the patchy distribution of the radioactive fallout and by the ways in which it was deposited. Rain water often swept it into the ground, and therefore it has persisted in the soil and thus in the food chain. The authorities who divided the land into three contaminated zones set a new 'lifetime dose' of 'permissible' radiation for those left living on the land. This was set initially at 25 Rem. This was altered in 1988 to 35 Rem. By contrast, the lifetime dose limit as set for members of the public by the International Commission on Radiological Protection is 7 Rem.

13

Operation Hope

WHEN WE RECEIVED that famous SOS fax appeal back in 1991, little did we know how much we would eventually immerse ourselves not only in the issue of Chernobyl but also in the lives of the victims. Little did I or Norrie McGregor, our Administrator, or our Cork CND Volunteers know what would unfold as a result of our initial response to that fateful fax message. What started out as purely a response to children in crisis has become a very comprehensive and effective programme of humanitarian and medical aid. Our work has developed in three distinct ways.

We organize rest and recuperation holidays in Ireland for children from the affected regions of Belarus and western Russia (to date we have brought 1,000 children). The value of good, clean air and nourishing food is encapsulated in the words of one of our Belarussian doctors, who says, 'The holiday returns to the children the gift of two years of stolen life.' They get a chance for their damaged immune systems to recover and their bodies soak up the value of healthy food, which we supplement with additional multivitamins. The children have become the greatest ambassadors for their countries' plight. Their presence helps to generate public support for our work.

In tandem with the holiday programme we organize a medical and humanitarian aid programme. In the past four years we have sent medicine to the value of $3.75 million to the Chernobyl-affected areas of Belarus, and we donated our first fleet of ambulances in the autumn of 1994. The medical aid programme has surpassed all of our expectations, and we are delighted to say that we have donated more than the United Nations special Chernobyl appeal. Not bad for a small country!

For the ninth anniversary of the Chernobyl accident,

'Operation Hope' was launched. The plan was to send our second fleet of twelve ambulances along with two trucks of life-saving medicines, including a 40-foot container of medical supplies donated by an American charity called AmeriCares. This involved a great deal of work, both in terms of acquiring and purchasing medicine and in the renovation of the ambulances. For this work we have a terrific team of ambulance-men and firemen from Waterford and Cork who work every spare moment on ambulance renovations. The team is led by Liam Grant and Dónal O'Sullivan, men who don't take no for an answer!

Ali Hewson and I went to Belarus in advance of the convoy to arrange the groundwork for its arrival. It was a pretty hefty task, given that the convoy was expected on Easter Sunday and everything, including the customs, was shut down. For once we were delighted to hear that there was a delay – the convoy would not arrive until the Monday. When they finally reached Minsk there was great excitement and enthusiasm, as people stopped on the streets, watching and clapping as the long string of vehicles slowly made its way to the customs compound. The lads took a day to recover and then split into several teams to travel to different areas with the ambulances and trucks. Finally, after seven days of travelling across Europe and eventually across Belarus, Operation Hope had achieved all it had set out to do. The aid was worth over $650,000, and within hours of its distribution lives were being saved.

We had 26 men in the convoy who had acted as drivers and mechanics and had agreed to go to Belarus as humanitarian aid workers for the Project. It is a well-deserved title for all of them who gave up their personal holidays to participate in the convoy. Six of the men were from the Waterford Crystal Factory and had been given the full blessing and support of the management. Between the workers and management at the factory enough money was raised to purchase and renovate two ambulances. Later on a video of the convoy trip, *Operation Hope*, was made by the Waterford Crystal Factory. It has been a tremendous promotional aid for the work of the Project and has encouraged other companies to give similar support.

In October 1994 our second convoy of the year, consisting of 14 ambulances and three trucks of aid, and valued at $1 million was sent to southern Belarus and western Russia. One ambulance was donated by the Welsh people, along with a truck of medical aid from our Project group in Manchester. This time the drivers included members of the Irish Army, Ali, the famous Irish journalist Nell McCafferty and myself. It was a long and arduous trip, and I sometimes wondered, as we slept each night for a week on boxes of medicines in the back of an ambulance, if we were quite sane! There were moments of complete exhaustion, and others of great fun and laughter. There were times when the pressure of organizing for 38 aid workers almost got the better of me. But by a combination of luck and determination we managed to keep the convoy together and to oversee the distribution of the ambulances and aid. It was a very rewarding trip for everyone, particularly Liam Grant and his crew, who had spent endless hours stripping down the engines and rebuilding the bodies of old ambulances. They were very pleased to see the relief on the faces of the doctors who for the first time had proper transport for their patients and a new supply of urgent medicine to administer and distribute.

We also place a huge emphasis on education. The Irish CND Peace Education Programme plays a vital role in educating young audiences not only about the Chernobyl tragedy but also about the dangers of the whole nuclear fuel cycle. The documentary, *Black Wind, White Land – Living with Chernobyl*, is part of this education process, and so too is this book. Our work on Chernobyl has truly shown the humanitarianism of the peace movement and has mobilized and empowered thousands of young and old people to take action. One of my proudest moments occurred when in my role as 'Grand Marshall' of the Cork St Patrick's Day Parade in 1994 I watched the first aid truck and ambulance (which departed for Chernobyl directly from the parade) pass the reviewing stand. It was surrounded by dozens and dozens of children dressed up as doctors, nurses and patients: children carrying children in stretchers; children pushing their dolls and teddies in buggies; all carrying little signs saying, 'Children saving children', 'Children healing Children', and 'Children Together'. 'From Ireland to Chernobyl with love' received first prize in the parade's environmental section.

Not only must great tribute be paid to our children but it must also be paid to their parents. Thousands of families all over Ireland

and England have opened not only their hearts but also their front doors and given the children of Chernobyl 'safe haven'.

And we're not finished yet! In the autumn of 1995 thanks to the American actor Paul Newman and the 'Hole in the Wall Gang Fund', we brought the first group of children to Ireland that normally had to be left behind. One of the saddest jobs I have had to do each year is to choose which children will come to Ireland, leaving behind the ones who are extremely ill or in their final stages of life. But now, with Paul Newman's wonderful offer of this European Holiday Camp for terminally ill children, we can bring to Ireland the children who are normally left behind to languish in their hospitals. Paul has been 'loaned' an amazing 500-year-old place called Barrettstown Castle, located in County Kildare about an hour's drive from Dublin. Formerly it was the Irish National Stud Farm. More recently it has been home to the world-famous cosmeticist Elizabeth Arden, and many of the rooms are still decorated with her favourite colour – pink! The Barrettstown Gang Camp is situated on acres and acres of lush Irish grasslands, woodlands and gardens. Many of the former stables have been converted into wonderful playrooms, work-rooms and arts and crafts rooms for the visiting children. The children are closely minded by voluntary Camp Counsellors. The children have an opportunity for enjoying life outdoors that would be otherwise impossible for them. Thanks to the Irish Government's generosity, Paul's and the Hole in the Wall Gang's dream has become a reality. The first group of Chernobyl children from southern Belarus and western Russia went to Barrettstown Gang Camp in the summer of 1995 and had the holiday of a life-time, along with excellent but unobtrusive medical attention. Ali and I met Paul at the opening of the Camp. His enthusiasm for it was very obvious. His quote in the Camp brochure sums up his enthusiasm and his sparkling personality: 'When I saw Barrettstown Castle, I knew that this was where I wanted the European Camp to be. I imagined a kind of Medieval Bazaar where children from different countries could raise a little hell together.'

The children of Chernobyl are also 'our' children and we should renew our personal commitment to ensuring that they, and the children of the world, are no longer threatened by radioactivity. As part of our on-going commitment to the people of Belarus we have 'adopted' hospitals and orphanages and we intend to send out consignments of supplies throughout the year.

The message we give the children to take to their families and friends is that we have not forgotten, we will not forget, and we accept responsibility for easing their pain and suffering. Instead of being engulfed by the magnitude of the problem, we have transformed the crisis into a source of inspiration and meaning for ourselves.

I think that the Irish response is perhaps a little unique and has its roots in what we have learned from our own history, when during the mid-1800s we suffered a terrible Famine. We lost half of our population through starvation and mass emigration. In our time of great suffering the hand of love and solidarity was extended to us by the Choctaw Nation of native American Indians. The Choctaw Nation heard of the plight of the Irish people and sent shipments of grain and corn to help to keep our people alive. During these dark times in Ireland the hand of friendship was offered to us when there was nothing left to live or hope for. The Choctaw Nation had been decimated 16 years before our Famine through their forced removal from their traditional lands in Mississippi to Oklahoma. When they heard of the plight of the Irish people it was an echo of their own experience.

Many legacies have been handed down since that time in Ireland, one of which is a deep and abiding compassion and concern amongst Irish people for those who suffer today. When we see images from crisis areas around the world we feel a deep affinity for the traumatic experiences of our fellow human beings. We know and recognize that their suffering was once our own suffering. Humankind is strong only when another people's pain and suffering is felt as our own. Chernobyl is stamped into the minds and hearts of the people for ever.

So when we heard about the tragedy of Chernobyl we immediately wanted to help to ease the burden of the victims, because we understand what it means to be without hope or the will to survive. The experience of working with the people affected by Chernobyl has changed my life. Not only has it changed my life but also the lives of many people that I have come in contact with. As a result of the Irish experience, branches have been set up in

26 centres around Ireland, in Manchester in England, in Derry in Northern Ireland, and in Boston in the USA.

I believe that many people have been affected by the work of the Project, which has received genuine help from a wide variety of sources for which I will be for ever grateful. People from all over the country have risen to share the burden with us. We even managed to get the Irish Army to help! It came about through Battery Sergeant 'Pops' Kelleher (one of our 'host' parents to the children), who was serving time in the Lebanon in 1995 as part of the Irish UN Peace Keeping Force. He managed to persuade 140 UN troops from Ireland, Finland and Norway to participate in a sponsored walk from 'Camp Shamrock' across 36 kilometres of desert to 'Camp Tara'. A novel and lovely way to unite such a trouble spot! Sergeant Kelleher's effort, along with a 24-hour 'radiothon', raised enough money to buy two ambulances. When our Minister for Defence, Hugh Coveney, heard of the initiative he sent a wonderful letter of support to the troops, and on the strength of the example of his men he gave us another ambulance from the Department of Defence which was about to be taken out of service. This ambulance has since been restored and renovated and is currently serving as a special monitoring vehicle used by scientists working in the radiation zones.

In 1994 I was invited by Her Royal Highness the Duchess of York, Sarah Ferguson, to give her a briefing on our Chernobyl work. The Duchess has a long-standing reputation for working with children under the auspices of her Foundation, Children in Crisis. As she is a frequent visitor to Ireland, she heard about the Chernobyl children. The initial contact was made in August 1994 on the day before our ambulances left for Chernobyl, a day of absolute chaos in the office!

Barbara, one of our key volunteers, was answering the phone for the day. She went pale in the face as she took one call which was apparently from the Duchess of York's office at Buckingham Palace. After taking down the phone number she hung up the phone, and we all laughed, thinking that it had to be one of our friends playing a joke (you'd be surprised at the number of joke calls we get!). After a small bit of debate we decided that I should dial the number and take pot luck. When the phone was answered, 'Hello, Buckingham Palace', I still believed that it was someone we knew putting on the most fancy English accent you ever heard. When I asked for 'The Duchess of York's office, please' and was swiftly put through to a woman called 'Hilly Bett', I still thought it was a joke. I was very casual and relaxed on the phone, as I was utterly convinced it was all a prank. As the conversation continued I slowly realized that it was real! The bottom line was that the Duchess wanted a copy of our documentary and as much information as possible on the Project.

When I eventually put down the phone I had to have a cigarette (I only smoke under stress!) and we mulled over the possible implications of the Duchess' interest. We put a pack of information together and sent it off. The response was quick and sure. The Duchess was more than interested. In fact she wanted to meet me, along with Ali from the documentary. I couldn't believe it! A date was set. Ali and I would go to London to meet the Duchess. We had a meeting ourselves beforehand to decide how best to inform the Duchess about Chernobyl and to suggest ways that she could consider helping through her Children in Crisis Foundation.

When we finally met the Duchess it was lovely, relaxed and special. I was very impressed with her honesty, integrity and genuine interest. If there was any difficulty it was only that it was a luncheon meeting, and I found it hard to take pleasure in the food, mind my manners and hold a conversation all at the same time! I was also a bit addled as to how I should address the Duchess. I eventually alternated between 'Your Highness' and 'Duchess'. I eventually relaxed sufficiently to tell her the story of Chernobyl, and any time I got a bit nervous Ali always kept the conversation going. We worked instinctively as a pair, just as we had when we were in Belarus.

By the time we were finished, several hours had passed, and the Duchess was committed to helping. Right there and then she made several proposals for on-going co-operation. I could hardly believe my ears. Her words were very genuine, and they have since been turned into action. Within two days of returning to Cork, the Children in Crisis office contacted me about sending out medical aid and taking children to the special 'clean air holiday centre' which had been set up by the Duchess in Poland.

In 1995 the Duchess brought together a number of organizations, including our own Chernobyl Children's Project and the

Chernobyl Children's Lifeline, to launch an international appeal for the children of Chernobyl, timed to coincide with the ninth anniversary of the accident. The appeal will last until 26th April 1996 and we have great hopes that the funds raised will not only provide medicine and equipment but will act as a vehicle to bring about public and political awareness to ensure that there will be no more Chernobyls anywhere in the world.

14

Return to Chernobyl

IRETURNED TO THE Chernobyl regions of Belarus in December 1994 to further research this book and to lay the groundwork for our next aid convoy. I was accompanied by Dónal Gilligan, the documentary cameraman, who took some of the still shots for this book, and Linda Walker of the Chernobyl Children's Project (Manchester branch). It was to be the hardest of all of my visits. What we found was a seriously deteriorating situation socially, economically and environmentally.

We returned to many of the villages were we had filmed in 1993, and what we found was heart-breaking. Many of the people whom we had filmed in villages like Tulgovichi had died, as had some of the children filmed by us in various hospitals and institutions.

The state of the deserted villages was also something we were not prepared for. On our return to Lipa, where we filmed the Day of the Dead, Dónal and I were shocked and saddened at the changes we found there. What had once been a beautiful proud village, even in its desertion, had been ravaged by unscrupulous, nameless men. They came brazenly to the village. Numbers had been crudely daubed on each house. Each timber, each window and each door had a number. The houses were disappearing. Whole streets were gone. It was a very disquieting sight.

As we stood in the middle of what once had been a lovely village, the silence was suddenly broken by the sound of sawing. I turned and saw a movement in someone's house. The three of us moved towards the sound. We stood at the door and surveyed what was being done. Two men were busy sawing up the floorboards. We asked them if they had the houseowner's permission.

'No,' was the gruff answer.

'What will you do with the timber?' we enquired.

'It is already sold, and when we have taken this house apart we will rebuild it somewhere else,' they replied.

'Do you know this timber is radioactive?'

They responded, 'Yes, but we don't care.'

'So who has given you permission to do this?' we asked.

We didn't receive an answer. They just shrugged their shoulders and gave a look which told us they did not welcome our inter-ference. They were pretty rough-looking men, and we took a risk in asking them any questions, so we accepted the signal they gave us and retreated quickly, wanting to say more but not daring to.

As we walked away the sound of their sawing filled the silence. I felt that a terrible thing was being done. This village had been like a burial ground, and these men were violating and desecrating this 'holy' place. What right did they have to do this? Unfortunately it appears that anything is possible for the right price. We were to find the same awful picture in all the deserted villages we visited. My mind flashed back to many of the evacuees we had spoken to over the years.

I imagined how angry and hurt they would be to see what was happening to their homes and villages. I thought about how I would feel if I was in their position – if it was my village, my home, that some unknown person came to, entered, stole from, numbered the bricks and timber, took it apart, took it away, leaving nothing behind to mark the 200-year existence of my home, my ancestors, my roots, my spirit. I would feel violated and angry. But for Belarussians there is no way they can vent their anger at the exploitation. There is only resignation and inward suffering.

And what of the people who will build their homes with the heavily contaminated building materials? No one knows. Someone later told us that these 'transplanted' homes were being sold as 'holiday homes' as far away as the Black Sea in the Ukraine.

We walked up to the graveyard where we had filmed. All the signs of neglect were apparent. No one had returned for the Day of the Dead in 1994. I now understand why. The pain of their village being torn asunder was too great. Standing at the ancient tree which dominates the graveyard, I looked down upon the sorry village. Not even the houses were left to stand in witness.

Where will it all end? My heart was heavy as I surveyed the village. I turned slowly around to face the graveyard. I could hear echoes of my last visit there – the welcome we had received, the vodka we had drunk, the bread we had shared with the evacuees, the tears we had shed, the old woman who had defied the guards and brought us to her house. Dónal and I searched the street for that house, but nothing of it remained. Everything, including the bench outside her house, had been stolen. Nothing remained except the memory.

Walking back through the village, we hoped to find the family we had filmed who had chosen to remain. With some relief we found the house still standing and some signs of life. We noticed it was the only house left in the village without its timbers numbered. For the first time we saw iron bars on the window of a Belarussian house. It had the look of being under siege. The dogs started to bark wildly when we tried to open the door into the yard. No one came to greet us. Perhaps there was nobody home. Perhaps they didn't want to see us. We wanted to be reassured that the family were surviving amidst this awful dissection of their village, but we had to leave with all of our questions unanswered and with our emotions in turmoil.

Our revisit to Mikulvichi was also rather strange. I breathed a sigh of relief when we drove through it – the houses remained intact. For how long I don't know, but at least for now it stood in all its beauty, covered in snow, watching and listening. Dónal and I had come to meet a very special old man whom we had filmed in 1993. I badly needed to meet him to feel reassured that some things remained safe and secure. It took us a while to find the house because we had approached the village from a different road, which left us a bit disorientated. And, of course, our last visit had been in brilliant sunshine, and now it was all covered in snow.

Eventually Dónal called out that he had found the house. When I joined him at the gate I knew by his face that something was wrong. Looking at the house, I saw the signs of neglect. The windows were clogged with dirt. The curtains looked shabby. There was no sound of the dog who was the old man's sole companion. We entered the house to find it completely empty. Memories came flooding in. The old man had welcomed us like long-lost relatives. The bottle of vodka had passed around and we had shared his scrambled eggs. Our laughter had filled his house with life, and now there was only silence. I was not prepared for the strength and power of the memories evoked. In this deserted house I was haunted by the spirits of people personally known to me. I remembered our dear friends Ali, Gerry, Liam, Dan and Isobel. I remembered sitting on the old man's couch, looking at the old photos on the wall, listening to Ali in the next room as she relaxed him with her voice before she interviewed him.

The old man was so proud of being made such a fuss of. He put his best hat on, grinning from ear to ear. He was so lonely that he was delighted to have company – and foreign company at that! He told us about how he had spent ten years in Siberia for a 'crime' that was never defined; how he missed his wife, who had died in recent years. God, how I missed him now, standing in the middle of his empty house with just the memories. Dónal took my photo as I stood staring out the window. He knew what was in my head and heart, because it was the same in his. In my head I whispered a prayer for the old man who had fed us eggs and vodka on a spring day in 1993.

I had a hankering to revisit Khoniki, where we had based ourselves during the making of the documentary. It was there that I had finally learned to feel what Chernobyl meant, not something that I knew intellectually but something that had become real and tangible. For me, Khoniki epitomized Chernobyl. It was the place where the crew had grown together with a shared understanding of the people's pain. We had all lived 'on the edge' in Khoniki. So returning there was very important. It was also the place where the authorities had the power to allow us to work or not. Negotiating with the same Mayor gave Dónal and I plenty of flashbacks. There was a lot of posturing, echoes of what we had encountered before. Eventually the authorities agreed to allow us, under armed escort, to enter the exclusion zone areas to take photographs for this book.

We didn't stay in the same 'wonderful' establishment that we had stayed in before, but one exactly the same just down the road. The three of us shared the same room. The toilet, shared with our neighbours, was a slight improvement on the communal toilet of our last Khoniki 'hotel'! However, it was an equally strange place and I have no doubt that the same kind of activities took place there! The place was freezing cold and we all slept with our clothes on. It was difficult to go into a deep sleep in the severe cold, and my mind rambled in and out of semi-consciousness all night. In this state of mind all kinds of memories came flooding in, and at times I felt unsure which year I was in. Was I back in 1993? Or was this another time.

The next day I was determined to find two boys who had spent the summer in Cork. I knew they lived in a village called Strelichevi very close to the town of Khoniki. The only problem was that neither we nor our guide had a map! All we could do was to hope that as we were driving along we would see a sign for the village. As luck would have it, we did! We were driving to Bragin and the guide announced that the village we were about to drive through was the one which the two boys were from.

At the crossroads we stopped to ask two young lads directions, and one of them said he would show us, so our guide invited him to hop in the back of the van. This boy turned around and it turned out to be Igor Smolsky, one of the boys I was looking for! He was beaming from ear to ear and was dead proud to escort us to his friend's house. We arrived in great spirits to meet Pavel (the other boy) and to bring greetings from Dina and Simon, his Irish 'parents'. Everyone in the family rushed out into the snow to greet us. I felt like I had known these people for ever. They brought us into the house, where we were presented with a beautiful wood carving made by the boys for Dina and Simon. We took photos and smiled a lot.

In the middle of all this I noticed that the house was very empty. Pavel's mother saw me looking and explained through Ruslan (our translator) that they were being evacuated. On the very afternoon of our visit the entire family were moving from their home to a flat in Khoniki, just three kilometres down the road. All their prized possessions filled one small car trailer. Chernobyl reality once again seeped in and spoiled what had been a lovely reunion. Pavel and his family would leave this village in less than an hour, never to return. If we hadn't arrived when we did there is every likelihood that we would never have been able to trace the boys.

Leaving the boys and their families behind, we came to the first of the three border posts which physically seal off the inner 'heavy' radiation zones from the 'lighter' zones. We arrived, under escort, at the first border post. Two soldiers, aged not more than 18, came out to check our paperwork. As we waited the 'officials' accompanying us laughed and joked about how well and healthy they were, despite all the times they went in and out of the 'purple zone'. My heart sank at their foolish, ill-informed comments.

The soldiers finally agreed to raise the barrier and let us through. We drove for a long time through what outwardly looked like a winter wonderland: beautiful forest covered in perfect snow. It was hard to imagine that what we saw was a great deception.

What awakened me from this wonderland was our guide pointing to a bus stop on our left-hand side. Across from the bus stop was a huge, ornate sign naming the village. But where was the village? Our guide swept his arm across a large tract of snow-covered land and said, 'There was the village. It is now submerged, buried beneath the soil and snow.' We got out of the van and stared at the emptiness that surrounded us. All that was left was the bus stop. A monument of sorts. Linda found some graffiti on it and Ruslan translated it: 'Valentina, my love – yours for ever and ever. Arkady.' Poignant sentiments. But where were Valentina and Arkady now, I wondered?

We drove on to the next border to find a very strange man indeed awaiting us at the fence. He looked like a cross between Rip Van Winkle and a hippy. He had long matted hair and a beard. He wore an ancient black coat which was held together at the front with a piece of twine. We hopped out of the van to talk to him and discovered that he had lived for the past two years in a small hut guarding the entry into the zone. Dónal looked in the window of this man's 'home' and saw nothing other than a bench, a chair, a table and some maps on the wall. He told us how he had come from Russia for this job and was grateful to have it. He was visibly pleased to have some company. We were the first Irish and English people he had ever met. We told him that we would come back for a further chat on our way out of the zone.

The final border post was guarded by a young man of 19 accompanied by an older man who told us he was from Azerbaijan. The older man told us that he was lucky to have this job, as he would have been without work if he had remained in his own country. They saw the geiger counter in my hand and asked me to check the levels inside their cabin. They were afraid that the levels were too high. They were right – the levels were very high. I wondered whether I should tell them the truth. In the end I showed them the readings, and they told me they were a little relieved, as the snow had dampened down the radiation, and the levels were lower now than they had been during the summer. The cabin was tiny and held little more than an open stove to cook on, two small beds and piles of wood from the nearby radioactive forest. They told us that no one could visit them and that they left their post infrequently, as there was no one to replace them. It was a very isolated place and an equally isolated existence. It was beyond me how these men survived.

Finally we arrived at the old village of Tulgovichi, a place that I had fond memories of. If you remember, this was the place where I got sick in almost every garden! When we arrived we discovered that only nine old people remained in the village. Dónal and I were anxious to meet the people we had filmed planting potatoes, one of the most beautiful and poignant scenes of the documentary. The accompanying militiaman knew the people and we walked up to find them. We were greeted with great ceremony. Of course the people remembered the crew. Yes, they recalled how ill I had been. I felt a bit embarrassed but the moment passed quickly as we asked about the others. We were sorry to hear that the woman who so kindly gave me the tea had died shortly after we had filmed.

In the middle of telling us what had been happening in their lives they brought out the famous bottle of *samagong* and insisted that we *chut chut*. As this was early afternoon, we were all reticent about drinking, but succumbed to tradition and the well-known Belarussian hospitality. We sat with the old people and asked about their lives. I felt so happy to be in this house, with life and love all round. I wanted to touch everything and know it was real. This was the way it should be in every house in every Belarussian village. But the reality of Chernobyl had changed all that. I love these people, and as we sat and laughed and talked, the bonds of friendship between us strengthened.

As dusk approached they invited us up to meet the other family left in the village. Leaving the house, I was struck by the beauty around us. The light was getting low but was wonderfully magnified by the brightness of the snow. We were all full of fun and laughter, almost forgetting where we were, as we slipped and slid our way past the empty houses. I was relieved to see a house at the end of the road where there were obvious signs of life – smoke from the chimney, light in the window. As we went through the yard the youngest member of the village came to greet us. He stood six feet tall, wearing a fur hat and boots. He cut a fine figure of a man in the dusk of the early evening. His mother joined him and we chatted about their lives.

As we were about to leave, Ruslan (our translator) came up to me somewhat embarrassed and whispered that the son had a fancy for me! I turned around and reckoned I had a wee fancy for him too! So we bantered back and forth about it. I 'christened' him 'Dr Zhivago'. Dónal the cameraman got very practical and announced that if there was any dealing to be done about me, it had to be agreed by him, as he was my 'husband'! Dr Zhivago was not at all perturbed by this announcement and cooly asked Dónal what would be 'the deal'. Dónal responded by saying, 'Oh, nothing less than two horses!' I was indignant at this and butted in, saying, 'I'm worth more than two horses! Demand a cart as well!' With this, my future 'mother-in-law' took Dónal by the arm, led him to the stable and proudly showed him the two horses in question and the cart. A bit of hand-spitting and back-slapping followed, along with a gift of a jar of honey and a bottle of home-brew *samagong* for the 'bride to be'.

Even as our militiaman and guide called us we were still carrying on 'the deal'. My parting shot was to say, 'We'll have a Spring wedding!' Dr Zhivago agreed. I waved frantically in between peals of laughter until Dr Zhivago disappeared. Poor Linda from Manchester didn't know what to make of all this, but I told her, 'Relax! It's just the Irish and the Belarussians testing each other's sense of humour!' The more I know of Belarussians the more like each other we become!

On our way out of the zone, we stopped and visited the man the locals called 'the Chief' and we called Rip Van Winkle. We offered him some packets of biscuits and the bottle of *samagong* as a small gift. His face lit up when he saw the bottle, and we discovered that he hadn't had a drop of alcohol for six months. He was thrilled with the prospect of having a drop or two and accepted the gift with relish.

Before we left we held a small ceremony at the exclusion zone fence guarded by 'the Chief'. I had been given a job to do, and on the spur of the moment I felt this was the place to do it. Many friends and children in Ireland wanted me to leave a message of friendship and solidarity to the people of Belarus. People who would never be able to take the risk and visit this place themselves wanted their support and care to be recognized. The question had been how we would do it. The answer came with remembering the Women's Peace Camp at Greenham Common, where people from all over the world had sent little personal items to be hung on the fence and left as a 'witness' and permanent 'presence'. So out of a bag Linda, Dónal and I took a variety of bits and pieces and tied them onto the fence. As we hung each item we named the owner and announced them 'present'. The little items included a baby's first shoe, a piece of child's favourite rag, a holy medal, a candle, a tiny teddy bear from Barbara, five Chinese worry dolls from Fleur, Fionnuala's bracelet, Deirdre's candle and a ribbon from her daughter Gisella, a painting of a rainbow and a letter to the people in the zone from a group of nine-year-olds in Westport in Ireland, and a white paper dove from my husband. As we went about hanging up this motley collection of personal things, the militiamen and the guards watched on with expressions of amusement and admiration. Despite themselves, they appreciated this gesture.

Coming out of the zone, we passed through the village of Novoselki. We saw children sliding up and down the icy road. We stopped to take a photo of a lovely horse and cart being driven up the village street. What a handsome, classic picture. Unfortunately this village would suffer the same fate as the others around it. Everyone was going to be evacuated over the coming weeks. The next time we visited this village it would be just another barren, empty, sad place.

Early the following morning we went to the local market in Khoniki. This was the place where people came to buy, sell or barter their produce. We met all kinds of wonderful people. When they heard we were humanitarian aid workers they queued up to tell us their story and to have their photograph taken. Amidst the piglets screeching we listened carefully to an old man who was one of the original 'liquidators'. He lived ten kilometres from

Chernobyl and the authorities had assigned him to soil sampling. He had no idea of the radiation and as the authorities sat in a closed vehicle he was sent wandering about the 'Purple Zone' collecting samples of soil. He dug the earth and used his bare hands to take the samples. He was never officially recognized as a 'liquidator' and therefore was not entitled to the meagre compensation received by the others. He was never given a geiger counter or protective clothing. He said that many other poor local farmers had been used in the same way by the authorities, who appear to have had little respect or value for human life other than their own.

We eventfully moved over to the so-called 'radiation checking centre'. There was no one in sight – no customers, which seemed odd, as every potato, chicken, pig, egg and plant was supposed to be checked. When we entered the centre we were made to feel very unwelcome and were bluntly told to get out. The reality dawned on us that nobody wanted to know what the radiation levels in their food were because it was all they had to eat. I looked across to the market stalls and saw throngs of people buying and selling. Would you blame them? Quite frankly, no. Their options were to eat the food grown in contaminated soil or to eat nothing at all.

We spoke to the butcher next door about the sale of contaminated meat, and he spoke angrily about how the authorities turned a blind eye to meat brought from the evacuated villages. It was supposed to be under strict control, but the reality was that it was not checked at all and ended up being sold and consumed by the people who came to this market-place. There was little or no monitoring. The butcher told us the meat was regularly 'mixed' so that nobody knew. He told us that the people of Khoniki were being used as an experiment. He added, 'The experts come and poke us to see if we are healthy. They never tell us the results.' This man came from a village called Dvorische which is only 35 kilometres from Chernobyl and has 650 families. They are still awaiting evacuation.

All these stories were proving to be very difficult for Ruslan, as he could not translate the sad experiences of his fellow Belarussians and remain unaffected. Taking us around the zone just re-emphasized his own Chernobyl situation. He was 23 years old and married to a young woman who had been so terrified of giving birth to their baby that she had a nervous breakdown after the birth and was committed to a mental asylum. Their tiny baby is unwell and Ruslan has to try and cope with this double tragedy in his life. Even visiting his wife is a problem, as it costs his month's wages to get a train ticket to the asylum near Minsk. He rarely sees his baby, who is staying with his mother-in-law near the border with Lithuania.

We left for Gomel late that day. Gomel is really the medical centre for the entire Chernobyl region, and in my view it has received probably the smallest amount of aid. A lot of the aid goes to Minsk, and somehow never gets redistributed down to the zones. The purpose of our visit to Gomel was to redress the imbalance and to discuss with local hospitals the possibility of sending aid direct to the area and to bypass Minsk. We already had an aid programme up and running with the Children's Regional Hospital, so this was the obvious place for us to start our work. Having been briefed about the deteriorating medical situation by Dr Rusakov, we were brought around some of the units.

We started off with the babies in intensive care – tiny little newborns struggling to survive. The doctor in charge brought us over to an incubator in the corner and said, 'That baby has survived because of the Irish ambulance given to this hospital.' Well, I was stunned! The story they told us later was that the baby was born in a remote village, and both the mother and child were in distress and needed medical attention. There was no transport in the village, and thanks to the recent donation of an ambulance from Mulranney, County Mayo, the hospital was able to collect both the mother and child and bring them into their care.

We eventually ended up in the children's ward and as usual we got engrossed with them all and took lots of photographs. As we walked along from ward to ward we came across some extremely ill children, and the distress of the doctor accompanying us was obvious. She told us that in former times these particular children would have been sent to Moscow for operations, but not any more. The two boys she was particularly talking about were quietly sitting in front of us on their beds. Their names were Vitaly and Sasha. I felt terribly uneasy that they should hear the conversation about themselves, but looking at their faces, I realized that they were fully aware of the life-threatening situation they were in.

Walking down the corridor, we heard the patter of many small feet running after us. One voice called out something to us. Stopping, we turned around to be faced with about a dozen children from the last ward we'd just been in. I sought the face belonging to the voice. It was one of the children whom the doctor had pointed out as extremely ill. It took the translator some moments before he could compose himself to translate. The boy, Vitaly Gutsev, aged ten years, had said: 'Please, please, take me to your country. I will die if you leave me here.'

To this boy's acknowledgement of his own death, silence was our response. My head wanted to disbelieve the stark words of the child. My heart told me it was the truth. A truth confirmed by Dr Edourd, who said in a very low and sad voice, 'This child is doomed to die.' Vitaly was in a very deteriorated state. His skin had a blue tinge to it; his lips, tongue, eyelids, palms and feet were black; the tips of his fingers and toes were already seriously clubbed. I shook my head and looked at Dónal and Linda. I felt powerless with the reality of this shocking news. I frantically searched for something to say. Eventually I muttered, 'Doctor, we will do everything we can to help this boy.' I didn't know if my words were empty and said just to console myself or if I really meant them. If I really meant them, what should I do now? The face of this boy would haunt me for ever if I didn't do something. I recalled other children I had known who had had very little time to live, and the aid I had sent had arrived too late for them. The children had died, in pain, forgotten. This time it would have to be different. I couldn't let Vitaly slip through my fingers. I had to try to save him. As we walked on down the corridor into yet another ward I started to devise a plan.

A seven-year-old girl named Evgeniya was in a special room with her mother. The doctor told us that they could not even diagnose her problem. Looking at Evgeniya was difficult, as it seemed like someone had run amok with a red marker all over her body. All of her veins were enlarged. Her immunity was very low and she ran constant high temperatures. Her body was very swollen from hormone treatment, and she looked more like a very, very old woman than a child. She had a very forlorn look. With difficulty we asked her to take off her pants and jumper so that we could photograph her body. It was hard to see her so naked and vulnerable, but we needed to be able to show the Irish doctors the full outward condition of her body. The child's mother stood at the bottom of the bed looking anxious and pale. She had kept a vigil at her daughter's bed on and off for six and a half years. She was tired and worn and had no idea what the future held for her daughter. As long as there was no diagnosis there could be no proper treatment.

Like every hospital we've ever been to in Belarus, the doctors and nursing staff were highly qualified and loved their patients. The grim reality of little medicine, poor diagnostic equipment and a continual increase in the number of patients makes their job almost unbearable. I have to admit that as we left the hospital I felt relieved, as I could hardly cope with the futility of it all. The three of us felt down in the dumps, especially thinking of the words of the dying boy, Vitaly. We agreed that we had to make some attempt to do something, and I wrote a fax to our office in Cork with a view to putting out a special 'SOS appeal' for assistance for the children. It took several hours to get the fax through, but eventually we succeeded. Nothing would probably come from the desperate fax that I had sent, but at least we all felt a bit better and less helpless.

Leaving Gomel later that afternoon, we took the road to new territory in the Mogilev region. The town we had chosen is called Byhov, which is situated in the heart of the second radiation zone. It was quite a distance away, but we were getting used to living in the back of the van, which became like a second home to us. The weather conditions were pretty severe, with constant snow-storms, but eventually we got there. We arrived at the local hospital, which received an ambulance from us in September.

One of the doctors took us around the hospital and told us how short they were of doctors throughout their region, as many young doctors refused to work in the zones for fear of the radiation. While this is completely understandable, it has put a severe pressure on the medics who have chosen to stay and help the people. The birth-rate in the entire region is now lower than the death-rate. This is a trend that has arisen in all the radiation zones.

We asked to visit some evacuee families but were told there were none in Byhov, as the level of radiation was too high.

The local deputy of the Supreme Soviet told us that he was a 'liquidator'. His task had involved evacuations, which had entailed 'intense persuasion at times'. He had worked in the Purple Zone of Mogilev over a three-year period. He told us how a large school had been built in the Purple Zone, and then it was discovered that it was highly contaminated. The school was never used. The Byhov area was declared 'clean' initially, but it was eventually admitted that it was seriously contaminated. Many villages in the area were demolished and the equipment used has been buried.

We visited the edge of Byhov's Purple Zone but were chased away by the armed police. They were only boys, 16 or 17 years of age. It was a very threatening and nasty experience. All we wanted to do was to photograph. They refused permission. Dónal got pretty annoyed and tried to argue rationally that we were there to help and that the power of the images he would take on camera would help the country through awareness, which would lead to international aid. But their answer was 'Nyet! Nyet!' and a long string of words that we were probably better off not understanding. We got the message! We left.

As we drove out through the exclusion zone we saw a herd of wild elk. These animals would once have been hunted, killed and eaten by the local population, but now they remained untouched, too radioactive to eat. Our guide, a local doctor, pointed to a lone building which was all that remained of what had once been a huge collective farm specializing in cattle rearing. It became so radioactive that it was eventually submerged under the ground. All around us was acre after acre of dead land. We passed a lovely orchard on our right-hand side. It was all that remained of what had once been a thriving village. The village itself had been buried. We passed many signs forbidding the picking of berries, mushrooms and any other living plant. I could not read the signs but I knew the radiation symbol. I could guess most of the content. As one old woman said to me in the local village when I asked her about the signs, 'Ah, when I see them, all I read is that we are sentenced to death.' I was numbed both by the physical cold and by the cold reality of the Belarussian people's lives. Lives that rotate around this restriction or that restriction. Go here but not there. Eat this but not that. Live here but not there. Die here but not there. 'What has become of us all?' I asked myself as we drove through what looked like the world's most beautiful spot, all covered in the purity of snow, with all the appearance of innocent innocence.

Exhausted by my own thoughts, we arrived back at the home of our host family, who were just so wonderful that the weight I felt in my heart began to lift. No one talked about what we had seen or experienced. We got the feeling that people were exhausted by Chernobyl. We respected the unwritten rule concerning what we could talk about. This young family had to live in the world's most radioactive zone and they had absolutely no other option. They loved their children and the mother asked if we could take her son to Ireland. I felt embarrassed by the plea because her son had already visited Ireland two years before, and because there are so many children who have yet to be taken out of the zones we have a policy of not giving the same children a second holiday. So with great difficulty I had to say that it would not be possible. She tried to accept my answer, but I could feel her despair and disappointment. It is the wish of every mother and father to have their children given such a chance. Unfortunately the numbers are so great that we will be asking our children and our children's children to take children affected by Chernobyl.

On discovering that we had no transport back to Minsk, the chief doctor offered us a lift in an ambulance. We gratefully accepted and hopped into an ambulance that said 'Mulranny Order of Malta' on the sides and 'From Ireland with love' on the front. We felt as if we were at home already!

We arrived in Minsk several hours late (due to a snow-storm) and just about managed to do a final television interview on why we were visiting Belarus. It was a difficult interview, and I would have loved to vent some of the pent-up anger and frustration I was feeling towards the authorities, but it would have been counter-productive. Instead I chose to pay a special tribute to the strength and stalwart courage of the Belarussian people. I finished with a message of solidarity and hope for the future and a recommitment on behalf of the people of Ireland to on-going support and help in the future.

After the programme had been recorded we left to spend our final hours with the evacuee families in Shabani. During the course of the evening there was a phone call for me from Ireland. It turned out to be my husband, Seán, who told me that the children were expected in Ireland the following day along with ourselves! I wasn't sure of what he was telling me, so I asked him to start again. Apparently the fax we had sent had made such an impact that our office staff immediately took action. The result was that the Mercy Hospital in Cork, one of our best local hospitals, agreed to accept the three children under the care of Sister Fidelma and Dr Seamus O'Donoghue. The only thing left was to get the children from the hospital in Gomel to Cork.

I was stunned and practically speechless (unheard of for me!) and just broke down in tears. I begged Seán to reassure me that this was a serious commitment. I was so afraid of giving the children and the doctors false hope that I had to hear it repeated a dozen times that the offer was genuine. I eventually got the message and ran back up to share the good news with the families, Linda and Dónal. There were cheers all round. We wanted to phone the hospital straightaway but refrained, as it was well after midnight. I was also afraid of making a promise and later finding some obstacle which would prevent it. When we left Belarus a few hours later our hearts were full of joy and we each had a great sense of achievement.

When we arrived at Shannon Airport we had to say our good-byes. Linda was off to Manchester, Dónal to Dublin and I was heading for Cork. Our parting was hard, as we had worked wonderfully well together and had been through what seemed like several lifetimes. We had done well and had achieved more than we had dreamed of. We each knew something very special had happened between us.

15

Bringing the children to Ireland

ARRIVING BACK IN Cork was easier than previous home-comings. I did not have the between-two-worlds feeling that I normally experience, so reorientating back to home life was not too traumatic. I was thrilled to see that Seán had made a special effort to make the house look good. He had even hoovered and put up the Christmas tree! It was lovely to be back to the safety and comfort of husband, home and friends. However, as it was the start of Christmas week I was all too aware that if we were to get the children to Cork for medical treatment early in the New Year, we would have to get it all organized before the holidays. Easier said than done! Little did we know what work was involved! But having a good team of people around me made everything possible in the end.

There were some anxious moments when it looked like every-thing was falling apart. One of the main worries which the doctors had in Gomel was that the children would not be able to survive the difficult trip, involving an eight-hour ambulance journey in freezing weather conditions, a two-hour wait at the airport in Belarus, a four-hour flight to Ireland followed by another two-hour ambulance journey to Cork. The parents of the children had a hard decision to make. Would they take the risk of sending their children to a foreign, unknown country, with the possibility that they might die on the way? Or would they keep them at home and accept their dying? Difficult questions. We could fully understand their dilemma and the responsibility that would be given to us if the children were put in our care.

What could we do to resolve the dilemma? Well, as luck would have it, I remembered an Icelandic businessman I had met at a Peace Conference in Barcelona. He had said, 'If there is anything I can ever do, don't hesitate to contact me.' I also remembered that this gentleman had mentioned that he owned an eight-seater Cessna aircraft! Bingo! The answer to our prayers! A private plan and an offer of help! Of course, it wasn't quite so simple. For one thing, the Icelandic man, Thor Magnusson, seemed to have disappeared off the face of the planet for Christmas week and couldn't be found for love nor money. I was being assisted by one of our volunteers, Barbara, who practically sat on the phone and fax for days, trying to track him down. Eventually we found him on Christmas Eve, about to board a flight from Heathrow to Iceland. We sighed with relief when he tentatively agreed. There was one major problem, however. His aircraft had been put in for servicing in Portugal for one month. Hearts sank all over the place. Were we back to square one? He asked me to give him 24 hours to come up with something. I told him I would wait by the phone.

True to his word, he called back later to tell me that he had arranged for another aircraft. Yipee! Screams all around the office! 'Sorry,' he said, 'not so simple.' He ran through the cost of getting such an aircraft – things like fuel, navigation/landing and handling costs. It all added up to more money than we had available. So it was back to the drawing-board. The only way we could quickly get money was to go to the media. A couple of calls later I had arranged with a freelance journalist, Maureen Fox, to do a full feature article on the story, along with an appeal. Our next breakthrough came with a phone call from Gerry Reynolds the head of the local radio station in Munster, 89FM. He pledged £1,000 from his special StatOil Christmas appeal fund. So everything started to slot into place, or so we thought. Nothing had prepared us for the problems arising at the Belarussian end. Major paperwork had to be done, such as passports and visas for the children. Getting the visas would involve an overnight train journey of 14 hours for someone, who would have to go all the way to Moscow to the Irish Embassy. Thanks to the dedication and determination of Dr Rusakov and his staff, all these formalities were complied with.

We were hampered by poor communications on the Belarussian side, compounded by the fact that we did not speak any Russian. So trying to get a complete diagnosis of the children's condition was extremely difficult. We were also running very close to the

Russian Orthodox Christmas holidays, which meant that our work had to be done in even less time. There were moments of pure panic, moments of frustration as we were unable to even get a phone line to Belarus, moments of tears and joy when we managed to get just another inch along the way. In the end everything fell bit by tiny bit into place. We had the complete co-operation of our Department of Justice and Foreign Affairs, and our Embassy people in Moscow can be proud of themselves. Take a bow, lads, you were great! They just waved a lovely magic wand at the usual formalities. I particularly appreciate the help they gave to the distraught mother of Vitaly Gutsev, who was unable to complete the paperwork in time and had to make a frantic journey alone all the way to Moscow, and arrived at the Embassy just as they were about to go on holiday. They waived all the rules and gave the visa for Vitaly. He was the boy who had made the heart-rending special plea in the hospital corridor which had set the whole ball rolling. It would have killed me to have had to leave him behind. Special tribute also to our airport authorities and to the national airline, Aer Lingus, who pulled out all the stops to waive all charges and treated the children on their arrival with special care. And thanks too to Sky Fuel in Ireland, the Belarussian authorities and the Icelandic people for waiving the costs of fuel and landing charges.

The flight was arranged for Monday 2nd January, which meant (or so we thought!) that Barbara, my assistant, and I would get a chance to celebrate New Year's Eve with our family and friends. Not so! Thor Magnusson had other plans for us which changed everything! On the afternoon of 31st December Barbara and I thought we were finally organized and were working away at our respective computers. Barbara was busily typing up a press statement, and I was absorbed in trying to write this book. Such momentary tranquillity was rare, and it was suddenly interrupted by yet another phone call from Iceland. This time the content of the call caused major ripples! The latest suggestion was that I should fly to Iceland to meet the President and to appear on national television to personally thank the people of Iceland, who had just donated 18,000 children's toys for the Chernobyl children's Christmas. Firstly, I was totally taken aback by the generosity of the Icelandic people, in particular the children; and secondly, the invitation to Iceland would play hell with my plans to have a relaxed New Year with my husband and family!

However, having discussed it with my husband, I decided to accept the invitation. So on New Year's Eve I found myself not out celebrating, but in bed by 11.30 p.m., as I would have to leave home for the airport at 4 a.m. on 1st January. I was to be accompanied by Barbara, who by this stage had become my 'right hand woman'. We both set off to Liverpool to meet a local Tory councillor, John Backhouse, who would bring us to Iceland in his private jet. John co-piloted for the entire journey and proved to be a kind and compassionate man. Flying in such a small aircraft was very exciting, and Barbara and I took turns in the cockpit. I had always wanted to fly an aeroplane, and I almost did on this occasion! Having a fascination about how things work and being curious about 'what if' I touched this knob or that, I found I had a dreadful urge to switch off the auto-pilot button like they do in the *Airplane!* movies and see what would happen! Of course, I never verbalized this tinge of momentary madness, and luckily enough the automatic pilot remained on automatic!

The flight to Iceland was terrific. Our only problem was not being able to go to the loo for five long hours! Barbara and I planned to rush to the nearest 'Ladies' on arrival. But, as luck would have it, we were unable to do so, as we were met by two television crews and a huge delegation as we stepped off the aircraft. Eventually we got some relief and had an opportunity to see all the wrapped and boxed Christmas gifts. There were mountains of boxes everywhere! The hangar hardly had room for any aircraft! When we arrived back at the aircraft at 4 a.m. the following morning we found snow-covered parcels all around the aircraft, left by unknown families for us to take to Belarus. Thank you, Iceland!

At this stage I thought the aircraft would be unable to take off with such a load. There was hardly room to breathe! And now that we had three extra passengers from two Icelandic television stations, there was even less room! Well, it was one way of getting to know each other! For five hours we sat huddled on top of each other, and finally we arrived on a beautiful sunny day at Cork Airport. We were greeted by my old friends, Mary Aherne and Anne Norman and of course, by Seán. When we had left Ireland we had left the others with a million and one little jobs to do, so after a quick report, lunch and a free refuel from Skyfuel, we were off on yet another long journey which would take us to the Chernobyl region of Belarus.

Thanks to Anne Norman, we had plenty of food, as she had prepared a pretty elaborate food-box to keep us going for the journey to and from Belarus. We swopped stories and got to know each other. It would have been impossible not to, given the fact that we were thrown together in such a confined space and for prolonged periods of time. Well, there's nothing like jumping in at the deep end!

Arriving at Gomel Airport in what seemed like the middle of the night was a disorientating experience. It was freezing cold as we stepped out of the snug aircraft and faced a group of approaching people coming out of the pitch darkness. Yes! I knew these people! Pavel, from our Gomel partner organization, accompanied by the Chief Doctor of the hospital, Dr Edourd Rusakov, and my dear friend Luda, who had worked so hard to make all of the arrangements on the Belarussian side. Amidst greetings and laughter we found ourselves being hosted in true Belarussian style. We all breathed a sigh of relief that we had succeeded with this very bold mission to airlift the children.

In the morning we left early to collect and distribute all of the Icelandic Christmas presents to the eagerly waiting children in the hospital. What a sight! We arrived with sacks of toys, and the children watched us with great expectation as we emptied the sacks on the floor of the ward right in front of the Christmas tree. It was such a joy to watch the children as they were presented with their gifts. Sitting down near the tree were the four children who were coming to Ireland. Three of them were sitting on their mothers' laps, and Vitaly, the boy who had the braveness to face his own death, sat with one of the older patients, as his mother was too ill to bid him farewell.

The four children shyly watched me approach. They were unsure of how to behave until Vitaly 'The Brave' (his new name!) threw his arm around me and landed a big kiss on my cheek. The 'merry band' had by now increased to four, as Dr Edourd needed the pacemaker of a little five-year-old boy to be checked by our experts. Chatting away to the children, holding as many hands as I could, eye contacting the quiet mothers, we eased our way into what would become a long-term relationship. These children were being entrusted into my care. It was an overwhelming responsibility to think about, but at the same time I felt it was a tremendous recognition of the trust and faith of the Belarussian people in the Irish. Many of the doctors and parents shed a tear as we embraced and hugged. We reassured the mothers that we would care for their precious children with all of our hearts and souls, along with our medical expertise.

At the airport the parents carried their children to the aircraft. It was a very poignant time. The little ones were wrapped up warmly against the freezing cold, held by their loving parents for their final moments together. Both the children and the parents showed worthy bravery as they separated, knowing that there was a possibility that they might not see each other again. We tried to make the parting as swift as possible, to minimize the trauma. I felt very emotional and had to keep on focussing on the fact that we were taking the children in order to try and save their lives. I had to keep working on the positive, or else my heart would have caved in. The words of two of the mothers helped me to get through the parting. They said: 'We understand that the next time we see our children it may be in a coffin.' With these words they had taken away my personal fears that the miracle we all so badly wanted might not happen. I felt released by the mothers' 'permission'. With these words ringing in my head, the door of the aircraft was shut.

As we took off, waving frantically, the children suddenly realized that they were flying for the first time! This revelation was a great distraction, and despite their grief they laughed and clapped as we lifted off into the clouds. The next five and a half hours had momentary difficulties, particularly for the little seven-year-old girl, Evgeniya, who was in constant pain. But we distracted them every so often with some food and funny stories. I slowly but surely enthused them about the 'adventures' they would have in Ireland when they were getting better. Vitaly was absolutely excited when he heard that Ireland was an island, as he had never seen the sea. So pretty quickly he started to look forward to his arrival. Of course, the key question for Vitaly and Sasha was, 'Will there be a television there?' And when I answered 'Yes' they were immediately sold on the Irish hospital! The children were accompanied by Dr Irina, a young pediatrician, who would stay with the children until after their operations. She turned out to be not only their doctor but a dear friend who was an important link between the children and ourselves.

During the flight Thor and John kept the children occupied by telling them exactly where we were flying over and at what height. Vitaly and Sasha had to know all the details and showed great curiosity about becoming pilots when they grew up. I will never forget that historic journey as long as I live. We were carrying the most precious cargo ever; we had carried off a miracle. I wanted to shout, 'Yipee!' at the top of my voice, but refrained when I looked at the sleeping children. Little Artem slept wrapped around Dr Irena, and Sasha slept in my arms. Whenever I could, I extricated myself to play hostess to everyone. I had always wanted to be an air hostess, and now was my chance! I served mushy two-day-old sandwiches and fruit juice to all on board with great style, despite the fact that I couldn't stand up and had to gingerly make my way over cameras and boxes to serve everyone.

Coming over Cork, I began to get anxious, as we were already running hours late, and my fear was that there would be no media willing to wait. I knew that media coverage would be crucial. But as we taxied up the runway all my fears were allayed, as I could see a huge crowd of dancing figures! I guessed it had to be Anne Norman and Mary Aherne leading the 'welcome dance party'! As the pilot opened the door and dropped down the steps, I peered out into a sea of faces. Yes! Everyone was there, including Seán, Fleur and Lydia from the office, the knights of Malta, and, of course, all the media had waited. As the children were gingerly carried off the aircraft there was a very special moment of hush amongst the crowd. As I crouched at the door of the aircraft holding Sasha, I looked around and saw that many were crying. The beauty, the vulnerability, the specialness of the children moved the crowd to feel great emotion. The children won the hearts of the nation from the second they were carried off the aircraft. As the doors of the ambulance closed I felt a 'whoosh' of relief that the 'miracle' had started.

I walked into the terminal building to attend our press conference. Sitting down and telling the story of what had happened since the famous plea by Vitaly made me suddenly very emotional. I fought back the tears of exhaustion and emotion and told of what we had witnessed in the hospital as we took the children. Looking around at the familiar faces of the media, I knew they would carry the story well and do justice to it.

The following day dawned to a blaze of wonderful photographs and television coverage. The children were now famous all over Ireland! Irish children started to send the Chernobyl children 'get well soon' and 'good luck' cards. There was also a constant stream of adults with their families coming to bring gifts to our children. Very soon their room became like a toy shop! Thanks to the endless patience of Sister Fidelma and her staff at the Mercy Hospital, everyone and everything was accommodated. The children were given a special room to themselves and quickly became the centre of attention with all the other young patients. It wasn't long before our young Belarussians were visiting boys and girls in other wards. Little ones next door started knocking at the window to attract the attention of the new arrivals. Very soon our children were settled into a loving and caring environment which would be crucial to their well-being and recovery over the coming weeks and, possibly, months.

Until this point we had not dared to think beyond getting the children to Ireland. Now, with that part of the mission completed, we were faced with the question of what we should do now. The children would need very specialized treatment which was not available in Cork, so we had to set about the delicate process of getting the children accepted into a hospital in Dublin. Yet again, everything worked in our favour, and with the help of Dr Seamus O'Donoghue from Mercy Hospital, within a week of the children's arrival we got permission to send the most urgent two, Sasha and Vitaly, to Crumlin Children's Hospital, which is Ireland's best children's hospital. We again asked for some favours, and thanks to Aer Lingus, we got the children, Dr Irina, Sister Fidelma and myself free seats to Dublin.

The day we left was the Russian Orthodox Christmas Day, and prior to the departure we managed to get a patient from the men's ward to dress up as Santa and to give the children their surprise presents. The children were genuinely not expecting anything, and the look of surprise on their faces was something else! Poor

Vitaly was not well that morning and was taking oxygen, while Santa, accompanied by a band of about 20 merry followers, sang and danced. Evgeniya, despite her pain, clapped her hands and sang all the words of the famous 'Kalinka', as Dr Irina took to the floor and showed us all how to do Russian dancing. We laughed and cried our way from the ward to the aircraft, while Tanya (a friend from Belarus who was married to an Irishman) played a very special tune of 'good luck' on her Russian accordion. She, along with our friends, stood on the tarmac singing and dancing as we taxied down the runway.

In Dublin we were met by my sister, Len, and my friend Eoin Dinan, who spotted us coming through the customs area pushing the two boys in their wheelchairs. The children were thrilled to see all the Christmas decorations and laughed at Len and Eoin, who were dressed up in Christmas suits. Despite the serious purpose of our journey to Dublin, we kept the spirit of Christmas going.

Settling the children into yet another hospital was no problem, as their lives had consisted of many hospitals. But Sister Fidelma and I found it hard to leave the children. We had even declared them 'honorary Corkonians'! Parting from them was harder for us than for them. The next time we would see them they would both have undergone very major surgery, and they would not have the smiling faces that we now looked at. But leaving them in the special hands of Dr Oslizlok and Mr Duff at Crumlin Children's Hospital, along with their medical team, was very reassuring. If anyone could provide us with a medical 'miracle', I was sure that these doctors would be the ones.

Moving Vitaly and Sasha took its toll on Artem and Evgeniya. The 'little family' that had grown together was split up, and the two left behind missed the others dreadfully. We had our first bout of loneliness when five-year-old Artem took out a little notebook with his mother's phone number in it and brought it to me with tears rolling down his pale cheeks, saying, 'Mama Mama.' He told Tanya that his heart would break if he didn't speak to his mother. We promised that we would try and phone her the next day, which we did from the pay-phone in the corridor. Armed with massive amounts of 50p and 20p coins, we eventually managed to connect mother and son. He cried and cried and told her to come '*zaftra, zaftra,* ('tomorrow, tomorrow'). Sadly, he was cut off and we were unable to reconnect the line, but we eventually managed to placate him. Artem took out his notebook every day and shed more and more tears, but thanks to the love of the hospital staff and the other children and their parents, he survived his stay in Cork away from his parents with great ease and comfort.

Eventually Artem was taken by Sister Fidelma and Tanya to Crumlin Hospital, where he underwent extensive testing. Finally he was returned to his 'home' at the Mercy Hospital, where he remained until he returned home to Gomel. The doctors have given him the 'all clear' and are quite sure that he will live a long and healthy life.

It is harder to talk about Evgeniya, the quiet, shy seven-year-old, who had to lie on her bed, unable to move because of her severe pain. Day after day I called to see her, and the more I saw her, the more I admired her. Despite all that suffering, she always managed to smile and to blow me a kiss when I would get up to leave and say *'Spekone noiche'* ('Good night'). I had a gut feeling that Evgeniya would end up being the saddest of all the children. It seemed that little could be done for her. The doctors started by reducing the steroids which had bloated her body so grotesquely and by detoxifying her of the cocktail of drugs that had been pumped into her over the short years of her life. The withdrawal wasn't easy. It increased her pain and made her even less mobile.

Every so often Evgeniya would ask questions like, 'Will I be getting better soon?', 'When I grow up will I be able to have babies?', 'Will the babies be like me?' Her constant, probing questions had to be answered without giving her the complete truth. Quite honestly, we could not fathom what could be done for her, but we had to believe that everything possible was being done and that it would at least improve her condition and at best cure her completely.

Evgeniya has a long road ahead of her, but she is armed with her own strength of spirit and courage. As I write she has started to slowly move around the hospital ward with the aid of a walker. With the best medical attention possible in Ireland, she is beginning to show tentative signs of improvement, which gives us all great hope. Dr O'Donoghue attends her each morning and gives her lots of time, affection and encouragement. I hope the miracle continues.

In Crumlin Children's Hospital things moved with great swiftness and expertise. The team of medics, led by Ireland's leading heart surgeons, Mr Woods and Mr Nelligan, were working towards performing major heart surgery. It involved extensive testing on both boys and ended up in a decision to operate on Vitaly first and later on Sasha. The children's deteriorated and complicated conditions caught the attention of all the medical staff at the hospital. Many times we heard it said to student doctors to look with great care at the boys, as the likes of their condition would not be seen again in Ireland.

I visited the boys only once before the operations, and it was a day I shall not forget too easily. A couple of days before the operation the hospital administrator, Paul Kavanagh, phoned me to say that he and the medical team felt it would be of primary importance that the two mothers of the boys came in advance of the operations. The logic was that with their mothers present the children would relax much more easily beforehand, and that in the crucial days in intensive care afterwards the mothers would be a key factor in the boys' recovery. I knew he was right and that, of course, the boys needed their mothers most of all, but I cringed at the thought of the mountains that would have to be moved to make it happen! As there were only two flights per week, it left us with only three days to organize the passports, visas and tickets. Not an easy task, when you consider that it normally takes months to get a passport in Belarus and even longer to get the paperwork for a visa sorted out!

But, as luck would have it, Dr Edourd and our translator Luda helped to make a special plea to the local authorities, and within 24 hours the two women had their passports. That only left the Irish visas. True to form, our Embassy were willing to waive the visas and to give a letter instead. But the mothers were so terrified that they would not be allowed out of the country without the actual stamp in their passports that they went off to Moscow on a 14-hour train journey to our Embassy. They were greeted immediately by Julian Clare, who gave them their visas within minutes. So the two women set off down to Belarus to prepare for the journey to Minsk Airport.

From there these two women, Tamara and Nazedha, left their country for the first time in their lives and set off to Ireland. They were greeted at Shannon by our ambulance-man Liam Grant, who drove them to Crumlin Hospital in Dublin. In the meantime I managed to get the train to Dublin, so I was there to greet the women, who arrived, appropriately enough, by ambulance! Well, the excitement was marvellous as the women arrived at the hospital, to be greeted by Paul and Eoin with flowers, smiles and kisses.

Almost immediately Tamara and Nazedha asked about the boys and when they would be able to see them. As we waited at the lift I could feel both the mothers' emotion and anticipation. Eventually the doors of the lift opened, and there were Sasha on a bed and Vitaly in a wheelchair. They were wheeled out to greet their mothers. Many of the doctors and nurses from Saint Brigid's Ward stood around and felt part of this very special moment. My own tears welled up as I watched the gentle reunion of the mothers and their children. The boys cried, the mothers cried, in fact it appeared that everyone shed a tear or two! It was hard not to get engaged in such a moment. We all discreetly left the four of them together so that they could have a private time to adjust to each other.

The mothers were overwhelmed, but nothing – not even their extreme tiredness – could spoil their reunion with their boys. That day is a day that I shall never, ever forget.

As the mothers settled into hospital life in Ireland the medical team prepared them for what lay ahead for their sons. Both Tamara and Nazdha were pale and frightened but were constantly reassured by Dr Oslizlok and Mr Duff that everything would be all right.

On 18th January at 8.15 a.m. Vitaly's operation started. He was on the operating table for many hours under the experienced hand of Ireland's best-known heart surgeon, Mr Nelligan. Vitaly subsequently spent time on the heart bypass machine. Tamara held an eight-hour vigil outside the operating theatre and practically collapsed when the operation was declared complete and successful. Her only words were: 'My son has come back from the dead. Thank you! Thank you!'

Vitaly was put in Intensive Care. It seemed like a million tubes were coming in and out of his body, but he had survived! Every second, every minute, every hour, every day that he now survived would be a strengthening indication that he would pull through. No one dared ask about his condition, but we all knew that his miracle had happened, and that there was every possibility that he would make it. Yipee! The whole country had been praying for him. Our phones in the office were ringing all day for news. The people of Iceland kept on phoning for news also. They had not forgotten the children, and I was asked to do several interviews on Icelandic radio to give the people an update. I was afraid to say too much, as there was still a long road ahead before Vitaly would be declared well enough to leave Intensive Care. He was over the first hurdle and everyone breathed a sigh of great relief.

Over the next week, little by little Vitaly started to come round. The blueness of his skin and lips started to fade and he became more and more like any other little ten-year-old boy. After eight days he left Intensive Care in his wheelchair and smiled and waved at everyone. Sasha looked relieved, as he could see that Vitaly had not only survived but looked wonderful! Seeing Vitaly so well and healthy was a great encouragement for Sasha, who would have his operation on 25th January. Since Sasha's operation had been postponed due to a slight infection, he had been fretting in anticipation of what lay ahead, and now he felt reassured and ready to face his life-saving operation.

In the middle of all this I received a phone call from the Foreign Minister of Iceland. He had seen the Icelandic news items about what had now become the famous 'mercy rescue mission' and wanted to know what Iceland could do. I agreed to fly out to talk with their Foreign Ministry and Department of Health. The Icelandic Minister for Health announced on television that he would invite other seriously ill children from Chernobyl to go to Iceland for treatment.

Two weeks after Vitaly's operation I collected him and brought him back 'home' to the Mercy Hospital in Cork, where he was put in the same room as Evgeniya. As he was recuperating we asked our rota of Chernobyl supporters to take him on short trips around Cork. He was taken to see the sea, which he had never seen before. His response to the most simple of things like shops, the river, swans and the cinema was a pleasure to behold. His face lit up with obvious signs of delight and his joy was passed on to everyone who met him.

And so it went on and on and on! No end to the miracles! The power of our love had overcome the most difficult obstacles and had strengthened, reinforced and regenerated all of us.

At 5.55 a.m. on 13th February I was awakened by a sudden, frantic buzzing of our front door bell. Half asleep, my husband and I looked out of the window and saw two strange men in our front garden frantically waving at us to open the door. Bewildered and sleepy, I crouched at the top of the stairs while Seán answered the door. One of the men identified himself as the night porter from the hospital. He said, 'Something is wrong with one of the children and you must come immediately.' Still not quite awake, we pulled on some clothes and drove to the hospital. I felt as if it was part of a dream. We were met by the Matron, who told us that Evgeniya had just died. In a daze of disbelief we went to the ward. A nurse motioned us behind the curtain that surrounded Evgeniya's bed. She lay there, in what looked like peaceful sleep. I thought I saw her move, but no – it was just my wish to see her move.

A strange sound came out of my mouth. My body seemed to be moving all by itself. I held her head in my hands and my tears poured all over her little face. I heard the sobbing of Seán, and I turned to him, silently mouthing, 'No, no, no, it's not possible!' I moved slowly around her bed, touched her hair, her body, held her hands, the hands that only hours before I had held and kissed in life. My God, what was happening?! I screamed inside for someone to wake me up from this nightmare that wasn't true. No one woke me, for the truth was that Evgeniya was dead.

She had died just minutes before our arrival. The nurses on duty were distraught as they told us of her last moments in life. It had not been an easy death. Finally she had given up the struggle to live, and so her last ten minutes had been peaceful.

Seán and I were joined by a very tearful Tanya, who had been Evgeniya's lifeline and solid friend. The three of us held each other for support, each of us locked into our separate but shared grief. We helped to take Evgeniya to the mortuary, where we sat and cried and intermittently touched her body. She looked so beautiful. Peace at least was hers.

We were in complete shock and disbelief. No one had expected her to die. Tanya and I had only just helped to wash her hair on

Sunday, in preparation for her mother's visit four days later. We had laughed and chatted about what her Mama would do when she saw her looking so pretty in the bed. Now, here was Evgeniya, laid out on a cold slab of marble, dead. We had moments of silence followed by crying and moaning sounds that seemed to come from somewhere else.

In numbness we left some time later and returned to our house to contact her parents and to arrange the funeral. In a daze I spoke to the undertakers about what we wanted for the church ceremony that evening. Tanya and I picked a white coffin and discussed what Evgeniya would wear. Later Tanya, Ann and I went down to the city to pick a white dress, shoes, and underwear. In every shop we told the assistants that our little girl had died. It was as if we had to keep on repeating the words in order to accept the reality.

We had to make a list of who had to be told and what had to be organized to get Evgeniya's parents to Ireland to recover the body of their daughter. We were dulled from shock and worked like robots. I had to sign an autopsy permission form and go to meet the doctor for the results. All this was done as if by someone else. I felt I had disappeared inside myself. Everything was done from a distant part of myself. I wanted to curl up, rock myself for comfort and let my inner grief escape, but there was no time, no release, no personal space.

Throughout the day people called at the house, offering sympathy and help. In the evening hundreds of people congregated in the Mercy Hospital Chapel for prayers around Evgeniya's open white coffin. She looked so lovely. The undertakers had laid her out in a Holy Communion dress given by a child from Cork. Her hair was bright and blonde and adorned with a band of white flowers. Her small hands were joined together and in between her feet lay her favourite doll, which she thought looked like herself. The priest, Fr Maoleas, called on me to share a few thoughts. As I stood at the pulpit I remembered how I had stood there only weeks before and had called on the prayers and good wishes of the congregation in helping to make the 'four miracles' come true for each of the children. I now stood before the same people in deep mourning for the loss of one of the children. Through my tears I said how I believed that all four miracles had been given, but we

140

just had not recognized that for Evgeniya her miracle was to be released from her pain and suffering. I spoke about the privilege and honour it had been for all of us to have had those precious five weeks with her. I said how wise and clever she was. I recalled how we had christened her the 'Queen' as she sat immobile in her bed for all those weeks, with great strength, acceptance and serenity. She had always been surrounded by her 'ladies in waiting', her dolls, who were rarely taken out of their plastic coverings. I recalled all of her probing questions to me about what life held in store for her, and how she had just four dates left to cross off her calendar before her mother came. The little girl who lay in the coffin before us transfixed in my mind the thought that love is the salvation of all of us. I thanked Evgeniya for giving us that gift of love.

After we had finished the prayers people filed past the coffin to see her just one more time. Some people placed flowers around her body. Others placed little personal momentos in the coffin. Most people just stopped, touched her, and came to offer condolences to Seán, Tanya, Sister Fidelma and I. We were all her family, and I felt honoured that people acknowledged that in such a traditional way.

The following day was filled with organizing for Evgeniya's mother to come here. As it turned out, her father was in Moscow, having just received the visa for his wife to travel to Ireland as planned. But by the time we contacted our Embassy, he had left and was somewhere in Moscow waiting to take his 14-hour train journey back to Belarus. We had no way of telling him that his daughter had died. It meant that Ludmila, his wife, would have to leave Belarus without her husband and without being able to share any grief with him.

When she finally arrived in Ireland the following night she was so overwhelmed by her sadness and exhausted by a new and unfamiliar world, that she was incapable of any communication. We brought her straight to the funeral parlour and led her to the quiet room where Evgeniya was laid out. Staring at her daughter, the reality seeped through. Her face and body contorted, she moved to the coffin. She paced around it, her hands moving every which way, her mouth uttering screams and incomprehensible sounds and words. Her screams lasted a long time, eventually turning into low wailing and keening sounds. Intermittently she would sit by her daughter, lay her head on her chest, stroking her face and hair, tracing the lines of her lips and eyes. She touched every inch of her child's body, all the while uttering soothing, gentle words of reassurance.

During this time I felt completely at a loss as to what to do. This woman was in torment, and I was so frightened by her grief that I was paralysed into inaction. I wandered tentatively in and out of the grieving room, watching, waiting, as if for some signal. I wanted to share my grief with her and tell her how I loved her daughter. But I could see that she was not ready.

Later that night we talked and cried together and shared photographs of Evgeniya. I told her all about Evgeniya's time in Ireland and how everyone loved her. She laughed when she heard about all the attention Evgeniya had got and she told us that 'the Queen' had always loved to be the centre of everything. As the hours slipped by and barriers between us melted away into understanding our mutual grief, Ludmila told us about a dream she had had in the early hours of Monday morning: 'I dreamt I was in the hospital in Ireland and saw Evgeniya running around the corridors. I called out to her and said, "Evgeniya, what about your pain?" She turned to me, and smiling, said, "Mama, there is no more pain."' Ludmila believed that this dream was her daughter telling her that she needed to be free from suffering and was allowing herself to let go. With this dream in our hearts we embraced and left Ludmila so that she could try to sleep.

As the body would not be cleared to leave the country until Thursday of that week, we suggested to Ludmila the next day that we should go through with all the plans that we had made with Evgeniya for her mother. Ludmila agreed. As neither mother nor daughter had ever seen the sea, it was top of the list of things Evgeniya had wanted her mother to do in Ireland, along with shopping for clothes and toys. The 'plan' was carried out almost with reverence, as if somehow Ludmila saw this journey as a pilgrimage in honour of her daughter. She rarely spoke, even when she laid eyes for the first time on the ocean that lapped upon the shores of West Cork. Pale as the white sand she stood on, she looked at the ocean longingly, lovingly. She cut such a sad, lonely figure as she scanned the power and beauty of the sea that spread before her. Every so often she wiped the tears from her eyes as she gazed at the gift stretched out in front of her, a gift that Evgeniya would never experience.

Leaving the sea, we went on to the city of Cork for the famous shopping expedition that Evgeniya used to talk about constantly. Ludmila walked through the city from shop to shop with little enthusiasm but with determination, accompanied always by her faithful host 'mother', Angela Burke, who minded and protected her. Having completed her pilgrimage, all that was left was the visit to the hospital to meet with the staff who had cared for Evgeniya.

We arrived at the Mercy Hospital and met with Dr O'Donoghue, who gently told Ludmila about Evgeniya's condition and the cause of her death. Ludmila listened silently, asking very few questions and seeming to shrink even further within herself as she looked around this place where her daughter had lived and died. She did not feel strong enough to visit the ward where Evgeniya had stayed or to speak to the staff. She told us that the spirit in the hospital was too strong and overbearing and that she was too weak to cope. She felt the presence of Evgeniya so strongly there that she had to leave almost without saying anything to the man who had not only medically cared for her daughter but who also loved her.

The next morning we arrived at the hospital chapel in time to greet all of the congregation coming to the funeral mass. The altar was awash with a wonderful array of colour and flowers. People from all over the country had sent bouquets and messages of condolence. Someone had left one beautiful red rose on top of the coffin and handed another to Ludmila. The chapel was full of the beautiful sounds coming from St Angela's College choir and the School of Music's string quartet. The place was already full of people, despite the fact that the ceremony would not start for a further half an hour. People moved around and mingled with each other, sharing stories about Evgeniya. Many of the people present had been part of her 'back-up' rota team and knew her very well. Others quietly walked around the coffin, stopping, touching it and saying a few private prayers. Others looked at the flowers, cards and letters, pointing out how letters from our Minister for Foreign Affairs and many of our parliamentarians were among the hundreds of letters from schoolchildren, families and just individual people, most of whom had never met Evgeniya but yet felt they knew her. She had somehow managed to embrace the country as her home and family.

As we sat all together in the front row, many people, including our Lord Mayor, Tom Falvey, and Bishop Buckley, came to pay their respects to Ludmila. There was a special atmosphere that morning as the chapel filled to capacity. The ceremony that followed was equally distinct, as it combined (I'm sure for the first time in Ireland) a Catholic Mass and a Russian Orthodox funeral ceremony. Fathers Maoleas and Stephen said mass together, interspersing it with the music of the quartet and choir. It was not only to be our final farewell to our dear young friend but also a celebration of the tremendous privilege it had been for all of us present to have had Evgeniya enter our lives.

A very special point in the ceremony was when, quite unexpectedly, Ludmila walked to the pulpit and, through Tanya, spoke to the congregation. She talked about how she had felt the love we had for Evgeniya and how grateful she was to the people of Ireland for giving her daughter such a special place in their hearts. Translating was extremely difficult for Tanya, as both women stumbled with their words through a haze of tears. It was a powerful moment, and as they both stepped down the congregation broke into spontaneous applause.

When both ceremonies had ended the coffin was carried out, followed by Ludmila and ourselves. It was only then that I fully realized the emotion that had been evoked in people during this final farewell. Everyone, even the hardest journalist, had shed a tear for Evgeniya. As we stood waiting for the coffin to be put into the hearse, Ann Norman arrived, soaking wet from the lashing rain, carrying a big box. She walked up to Ludmila, and crying (this was the first time I had ever seen Ann weep), she gave her the box, which contained the Barbie house that Evgeniya had always wanted. Ann told Ludmila that it was meant to be a dream come true, and that she had promised Evgeniya the day she had arrived that she would get her the Barbie house. Ann had planned to give it to her the day Ludmila was to come to stay so that they could share the excitement together. Ann asked Ludmila to take it to Belarus and give it to her niece, whom Evgeniya had often talked about.

As we sat at the airport, waiting for Ludmila's flight home, she started to speak in great floods of words. She told us that she wanted to help us in our work in the name of her daughter, so that others would not have to suffer and die like her. She asked me to come and visit her when I was next in Belarus. My heart lightened as she offered us the hand of friendship. All of a sudden it was as if her life had returned to her, and she quickly started asking about how she could help in the future. I was so grateful to her for this offer of support in the middle of her grief.

As we sat talking and making plans, we were honoured when our Minister for the Environment, Brendan Howlin, came to pay his respects. He had just arrived at the airport and insisted on delaying his itinerary to come and talk to Ludmila. Gestures such as this were so appreciated by all of us.

As the aircraft took off, we stood huddled together, crying and waving to Evgeniya on her final journey home.

Seán and I had decided that we should continue in the traditional style of an Irish funeral, and threw open our house for a 'wake'. We invited the entire congregation, and practically all of them came! The house was full of life when we returned from the airport, and the affair went on into the small hours of the following morning. We all needed to unwind and none of us wanted to be alone that night, so bodies slept where they fell. The following morning we woke to discover that the house had been burgled as we all lay asleep. But we didn't care! In the greater scheme of things, what did it matter?

In the days that followed we slowly pulled ourselves together. Two weeks after Evgeniya's death Ann Norman, Vitaly and I set off for Iceland to meet the President, who wanted us to share in the Icelandic celebration of Vitaly's new-found life. As we flew over the ocean Ann and I spoke about how much we both needed to recapture the joy of the other three children, whose lives had been saved, and Iceland was to give us that opportunity. We spent a week there as special guests of 'Peace 2000' and the Icelandic people, who welcomed us with open arms. Vitaly was a celebrity there, as everyone had been following his progress since the day Thor Magnusson had airlifted the children to Ireland. During our week we met the President, Vigdis Fingvogadottir, a woman well known for her love of children, and she gave Vitaly her complete attention. Vitaly was very proud to meet her, and was especially pleased when she gave him a special message of support to take back to the children of Chernobyl.

Other meetings in Iceland included talks with the Chief Doctor and the Minister for the Environment, who were very supportive of our work. As a result I believe our two islands will come together to combine efforts to help the victims of Chernobyl.

Since our return to Ireland Vitaly has been discharged permanently into our care. He returned home at the end of March 1995 with the happy prognosis of another 30 years of life ahead of him, thanks to the people of Ireland. Sasha has had a further two operations, and while awaiting another major heart operation returned to Belarus in April 1995. His journey for a longer life is not over, but he has survived the worst hurdle and waits, along with all of us, for his full miracle to come into being.

Before the arrival of our convoy to Belarus in April 1995 I made a very quick visit to Gomel to meet with Sasha, Vitaly, Artem and their families. Within minutes of my arrival I was surrounded by everyone and we greeted each other as old friends. There was much speech-making with strong words of gratitude to the Irish people. The most special words for me came from Vitaly's father when he stood up and said, 'I can die now because my son lives, thanks to the people of Ireland.'

While my visit to Gomel was full of the celebration of the boys' recovery, it was also filled with great sadness. Part of the reason why I had come to Gomel again was to visit an orphanage in the second radiation zone which I had heard about by reputation only. I visited it on my second day. It lay hidden away, miles from the city, near a small, poor village. As our van pulled up outside, I immediately knew that this would be a place for which we would have to make a crisis response. The 160 children there were forced to live in what can only be described as a barn – an old timber building with no toilet or hot water. Parts of the outside structure were falling down, and the windows were ill fitting and rotten. I could hardly imagine what it would be like in the severe depths of a Belarussian winter. This place had no medical facilities for the children and was totally dependent on the generosity of the already impoverished village nearby. We spoke to the director of the orphanage, who pleaded for help. He was a kind man who wanted the best for the children in his care, but with few or no resources, the children's future was bleak. He spoke about the growing number of children being abandoned into his care from the surrounding villages. People were losing faith in their future. The all-too-familiar story was being reinforced yet again.

Luckily, I was accompanied by a cameraman – Michael Kenny from the Waterford Glass Factory – who captured on camera the suffering of the children and staff. I promised to send aid within weeks of my return and to invite a large group of the children to Ireland for a holiday. Michael hoped to persuade his co-workers and management to 'adopt' this place and to rebuild it. With the power of his images and my words, I believe that this awful, sad place will soon be bulldozed into the ground and that the children will be given proper care. With my heart and head full of this bleak spot, I left Gomel to return to Minsk, where I was joined by Ali. Our joint task was to help with the distribution of the aid and to lay the groundwork for our next convoy.

Before I had left for Belarus I had been warned by my co-director, Ann Norman, to keep my mind on the business of the convoy and to be sure not to make any commitment to bring any more very ill children to Ireland, as we had enough to be getting on with already. I had solemnly promised her, 'Have no worries, Ann. I'll just focus on the aid and the invitations for the summer.' Well, I'm afraid I broke that agreement when visiting our old friends in the Children's Home in Minsk, where we had found 'small Igor' in 1991. This home for abandoned children has been transformed by the staff and now is truly a 'safe haven' for these special children.

During our filming in 1993 we had been refused entry into the adult mental asylum, where the children end up after the age of four. When Ali and I returned and enquired from the doctors about various children whom we had met in 1991, we were both distressed to hear that all of them, except two, were either dead or already in the mental asylum. The little girl that Ali was most relieved to hear about was three-year-old Nastiya, a beautiful child whom Ali had taken to her heart when filming in 1993. As luck would have it, she was still in the home. Out of sheer desperation and fear for Nastiya's future, the doctors appealed to us to take her, along with another little girl, Lena, to Ireland and save them from the asylum. Lena was already five years old and should have been admitted to the asylum. She had only avoided admittance because her protectors kept postponing the date of her departure. However, the staff knew that they were living on borrowed time and felt that her departure was imminent. We were their only hope. So anxious were the staff for us to help that they somehow managed to arrange for us to visit the asylum and see for ourselves the fate that awaited the children.

We arrived at the asylum early the next morning and very quickly realized that this place was hell on earth for those who had the misfortune to be committed there. It was like stepping back in time. There were moments when I felt as if we were visiting one of the death camps of the Second World War. The inmates were dressed in baggy striped suits and hats. They shovelled gravel back and forth in what seemed like dull oblivion. Theirs were the forlorn faces and shrunken bodies of people who had been just forgotten by the world.

We eventually found the children's section: a large, two-storey, run-down, foreboding-looking building. As we stood in the waiting area, we were all wondering silently what to expect. Our silence was soon broken by several children of various ages and disabilities who came among us, expressing great curiosity. As we moved to the second floor, I immediately observed the very poor condition of the interior. Floors were in need of repair, windows needed to be replaced, ceilings needed to be replastered. We walked into the first room, which had ten cots. I was struck immediately by the sound of the children: a disturbing cacophony of physical and emotional pain. As we filled the room with our physical presence (there were 14 of us), the sounds became even more frantic. It was as if the children knew we were there to help, and they were making one gigantic effort to make sure that we understood their situation. Our aid workers instinctively knew what to do, and each moved to the children, offering soothing words and stroking motions. Within seconds the sounds of desolation were transformed into sounds of comfort. Each and every child responded with as much outward sign of acknowledgement as he or she could.

These children lie all day every day in their cots because of the lack of facilities, their bodies wasting away. These forgotten children have never felt the grass, touched a river or seen a bird, because there is no transport. Their lives are devoid of any beauty. They are helplessly confined to cots, which are later replaced by beds, which are later replaced by coffins. The lives of these children are simply one long waiting for death. They are left in obscurity, isolation, hidden away.

The lads wept openly as we moved from one endless room to another. We eventually came to a room with a half door. Looking over it, we discovered twelve children. Some of them were moaning pitifully, banging their heads against the wall, the floor, the radiator, rolling around the floor in individual emptiness; children as young as two years of age but who looked and acted like ancient, demented, lost souls.

We came out of that place in a haze of disbelief at what we had witnessed. I now fully understood the distress of the doctors in the Children's Home and vowed to myself that I would rescue the two girls from this awful place.

On my return to Cork I broke the news to Ann Norman, who immediately responded, much to my relief, with understanding and support. Over a period of months, with the help of our Government, we worked to bring the girls to Ireland to start a new life. Finally we got the 'all clear'. To our great delight, when we were returning from our October 1995 convoy trip I had the great pleasure of going to the Number 1 Home and sweeping Lena into my arms and taking her for long-term care to her new 'Mama and Papa', Mossy and Noreen Canty in Ireland. We are still awaiting permission to take Nastiya, and hopefully that day will come soon. Having the girls is a huge commitment, as both of them need tremendous physical and mental help. But given the endless supplies of love and compassion which they receive from their 'families', their futures are looking bright and rosy.

And so I believe in miracles! Long may they continue! Through this work I have learned the great truth which is hidden in our minds and written in our poetry and song – which is that love conquers all. A love which is bountiful and boundless for ourselves and one another. A love which involves some personal cost, but the growth and wealth of spirit which one receives far outweighs the cost. A love which motivates us to protect the greatest gift of all – life – and to celebrate it.

16

The next Chernobyl will be Chernobyl

SINCE THE ACCIDENT, Central and Eastern Europe have undergone momentous political changes. The USSR no longer exists. Chernobyl is now the responsibility of the Ukraine alone. But the fallout from Chernobyl continues to kill and the reactors themselves continue to operate. Despite all the words that have been written about the accident, little has changed for the better. In fact in many ways the situation is getting worse.

For the first four years after the accident no information was available to the general public, and whatever information was available remained exclusively within narrow scientific circles. Only now is the chilling reality starting to unfold. We are not finished with Chernobyl. The scientists admit that the cement 'Sarcophagus' which encases the damaged nuclear reactor is now cracking open and leaking out lethal doses of radiation. Holes and fissures in the structure now cover 1,000 square metres. Some of these holes are large enough to drive a car through. These cracks and holes are further exacerbated by the intense heat inside the reactor, which is still over 200 degrees Celsius. The Sarcophagus' hastily and poorly built concrete walls are steadily sinking.

The scientists now agree that this Sarcophagus will eventually collapse, and when it does there will be an even greater release of radioactivity than in the initial accident in 1986. Twenty thousand tons of concrete floor is about to collapse into what can only be described as a mix of radioactive lava and dust, which resulted from the dropping of tons of sand in the early attempts to put out the fire. Will the international community help to prevent this collapse from happening?

We have a responsibility to ensure that this crime against humanity is not allowed to continue. We must demand that our respective governments take action within such fora as the UN and the EU. The people of Belarus cannot afford to be exposed to 'Chernobyl 2', because they are already being constantly recontaminated through the food chain.

This tomb which was to last for eternity began to disintegrate within five years. Dealing effectively with the aftermath of Chernobyl involves far more than the entombing of the reactor. Even a second sarcophagus built with the latest technology would still be guaranteed to last only 100 years. Moreover, the problem is compounded by the inability of the Ukrainians to deal adequately with any further crisis that may arise at the site. Since the break-up of the USSR, most of the Russian scientists and experts have left, and there is little cross-border co-operation over the problems of Chernobyl. The Ukrainians have been deserted by Russia and are operating the Chernobyl reactors without adequate equipment and necessary expertise.

The pillars supporting the building which contains the damaged reactor are in serious danger of bursting. If this is allowed to happen, the consequences could include the crashing of debris right through the concrete Sarcophagus; or rubble could lunge into the fully functioning Reactor 3 which is right next door. This could trigger a core meltdown which would send another radioactive plume into the atmosphere, and this plume would subsequently blow all over Europe. There are 740,000 cubic metres of lethally contaminated debris inside the Sarcophagus, which is ten times more debris than was previously thought.

The report which reveals this vital information is being concealed by the European Commission, which is arguing with the Ukrainians over who will foot the bill for the Chernobyl clean-up operation. Every day lost to political haggling increases the possible risk of nuclear debacle. If this situation is allowed to continue, what we can expect some time in the future is an explosion that will destroy not only the immediate territory of the affected countries, but also an extensive area of Europe.

The European Commission sponsored the report because of its justified fears relating to the state of the Sarcophagus, but it made a concerted effort to force engineers and scientists to withdraw a whole chapter when it realized the full-scale nightmare of the

Sarcophagus' condition. In March 1995 the report's findings were presented to a group of international experts sworn to secrecy. 'So alarming were the conclusions that press conferences scheduled for Paris and London were abruptly cancelled,' said *The Observer* on 26th March 1995. The newspaper had obtained a copy of the report and gave it front-page coverage.

Georgyi Kopchinsky, the Ukraine's second most senior nuclear regulator, resigned in late November 1993 because he could not accept the Ukrainian parliament's decision to keep the Chernobyl nuclear power plant operating indefinitely. The parliament voted on 20th October 1993 to lift the moratorium on constructing new reactors and also to allow Chernobyl 1 and 3 to continue operating and to possibly restart Chernobyl 2. It reversed a 1991 decision that the entire station would be shut permanently on 31st December 1993.

Kopchinsky is said to have spent long hours explaining the safety problems to government and parliament officials. 'I don't understand their decision,' he said. 'The situation in the Ukraine today is very similar to the situation in 1985–86 which led to the Chernobyl accident.' Yet despite his protests, the parliament decided that Chernobyl 2, whose turbine was badly damaged in an October 1991 fire, could be put back into operation.

In October 1994 the EU finally put pressure on the Ukraine to close Chernobyl, and it may well pay off. The Ukrainian Foreign Minister, Hennady Udovenko, assured a meeting of EU foreign ministers that the Ukraine was committed to closing the plant. This new declaration should unlock some 500 million ECUs of EU funds and a further £200 million from the Group of Seven major industrialized countries.

Until this point no one knew if the Ukraine would make such a commitment to close the plant. However, the task will be far from easy. It is clear that the sums of money needed will be far greater than what the EU has put on the table. No one knows who will provide the rest of the funding.

The EU are adamant that the plant must close and have advised the Ukrainians that it is 'non-negotiable'. The German Foreign Minister, Klaus Kinkel, left his Ukrainian counterpart in little doubt about his feelings on the closure: 'I have one clear statement: Chernobyl must be shut down. It will not be easy because of Ukraine's energy needs, but the risks are just too great.' Let's hope that these fine words transfer into both real and immediate action before it is too late.

The European Commission report must be heeded and should not end up gathering dust on some shelf in Brussels, leaving Chernobyl teetering on the brink of a major calamity. Experts agree that it will take at least 100 years to complete the Chernobyl clean-up. According to Dr John Large, a leading British independent nuclear safety expert, Chernobyl's debris will be radioactive for hundreds of thousands of years and must be treated and buried in shallow graves as an urgent priority. Meanwhile the Chernobyl time-bomb is ticking away as politicians lock themselves into arguments about who will pay. But what price will we pay if nothing is done? It appears that economics and politics take priority over human safety.

There is little doubt that the Sarcophagus is sinking into the ground. 'There are simply no proper foundations,' says German radiobiologist Professor Edmund Lengefelder. This giant concrete shell is falling apart and casts a dark shadow over this already gloomy picture. It is a graphic symbol of the nuclear monster that is not willing to lie down and die. The cost of replacing it is undoubtedly a problem, but to do nothing would be unthinkable and unforgivable.

The Chernobyl disaster represents the first large-scale 'experiment' in the management of a nuclear crisis, and it has failed miserably. It has had a social impact unparalleled in human history. People's view of nuclear technology has been changed for ever. The accident that scientists were so convinced 'could never happen' has marred the lives of millions and caused the devastation of what was formerly known as 'the bread-basket of the Soviet Union'. The scientists were paralysed into inactivity by their own deception. It was as if to admit to the accident was an admission of defeat. The scientific community must now recognize that the human body's response to radionuclide pollution is far more serious than ever imagined by the nuclear industry. We have not developed resistance to natural or man-made radioactivity. Nuclear science has even created new radioactive elements such as plutonium and caesium which had never before existed on the living planet.

153

The magnitude of the accident has not been grasped by the international community. Not only were the predictions of the health effects grossly incorrect, but no one is seriously looking at the incalculable damage to the victims both emotionally and psychologically. This is not a calamity where people are dying in the streets of towns and villages. It is a tragedy where thousands of families and communities are quietly suffering, their lives constantly disrupted by ill health and personal crises. Worst of all, they are fearful about their futures and about having to prepare to leave their homes at any time. Their lives have been corrupted by the nuclear cloud that hangs over them every day. We have entered an era of nuclear violence, a global sickness of endless destruction. How many Chernobyls can the planet endure? This tragedy is a stain on human history.

One of my strongest memories of being in the zones is a constant sense of mourning and grieving both for the people and for the land. Every part of the life-cycle has been damaged, from the unborn to the aged and everything in between. Quite apart from the health and environmental effects, just the sheer monetary cost of Chernobyl provides us with the most powerful argument against further nuclear development. The cost of Chernobyl is several billion dollars, a cost which will have to be carried by the survivors and their children over the coming decades. It is a legacy of misery to be passed on from generation to generation, among a people who have already paid too high a price.

The Chernobyl cover-up is still very much in place. The chaotic economic situation of Belarus means that only limited information is available to us. The government is trying to entice multinational companies to invest in the country, so the whole Chernobyl question is brushed under the carpet, as they are fully aware that companies would not consider setting up in Belarus if they were to be made fully aware of the environmental damage to the country as a whole. Economy with the truth is a problem which is further compounded by a relatively unchanged political situation.

We need to grasp the international dimensions of the accident and the global nature of its implications. The constant radioactive degradation of our human habitat has to be addressed. The Chernobyl accident belongs to the saddest chapters of the *Guinness Book of Records*. Ever since Hiroshima and Nagasaki our civilization has had to face a steady degradation of our habitat as a result of artificially created radiation. The world community must respond and prevent potential and also existing environmental radiation crises. Environmental hazards caused by radiation are already a fact of life and right now jeopardize the future of a whole nation. The accident poses a crisis of science, and the transboundary nature of the consequences must be addressed. If we don't join together and honestly face the catastrophe to ensure that it does not occur elsewhere in the world, the whole of humanity will suffer a truly irreparable tragedy.

Ten years after the accident it is obvious to everyone that the radiation did not stop at the Ukrainian border. The consequences have been felt worldwide. One of the least known consequences has been the distribution of contaminated agricultural products. Much of the food has been dumped on southern hemisphere countries, usually countries in great need of food or without adequate import control facilities. Some of this contaminated food, unacceptable for northern hemisphere consumption, went as 'aid'. Such actions are both immoral and criminal. Contaminated meat has become so common in West Africa that port authorities have forbidden the import of all EU meat. Such scandalous activities must be not only condemned but stopped.

The principle of learning from mistakes cannot be applied to nuclear reactors. The potential for enormous disaster is too great, and both numbs and defies the imagination. Not only is the technology highly dangerous, but we must take human fallibility into account. If we truly love this planet we will need to change our nuclear addiction habits. Humanity sits under the shadow of the mushroom cloud. All of our lungs and bones are daily threatened by radioactivity.

Yet we declare today our hope in the future. From the diversity of all of our heritages and cultures we renew our belief in the holiness of the earth and the sanctity of all life. Our task is to release ourselves from the bondage of old patterns of thinking which try and tell us what we need security for and defence against. I believe in my heart and in my soul that the earth's security rests not in the accumulation of weapons of mass destruction but in justice. In the justice of adequate housing and food; in the justice of an economic system that gives us access to what the earth has in abundance; in the justice of meaningful education and work; in the justice of safe, clean and renewable forms of energy. Before us today are set two things: life and death. Let us celebrate in our choice of life so that we and our children may simply live. That is our task for the future.

My life-blood is sustained and maintained in working with children, our hope for the future. It is in their name that I commit myself to working towards changing the minds and hearts of humanity to recognize the 'connectedness' of all life. It appears to be difficult for humans to comprehend that all things are truly interdependent and interconnected. Just as it was hard for humans to accept the discovery that the earth was not the centre of the solar system. So I take heart in the knowledge that eventually we learn to accept new concepts and teachings. I am nurtured, empowered and challenged for the work that needs to be done by the prophetic message given to us in 1854 by Chief Seattle, when he surrendered Indian land in the territory of Washington to the US Government. This was his message:

> The shining water that moves in the streets and rivers is not just water, but the blood of our ancestors. If we sell you our land, you must remember that it is sacred and you must teach your children that it is sacred . . .
>
> The rivers are our brothers, they quench our thirst . . .
>
> The air is precious to the red man, for all things share the same breath – the beast, the tree, the man, they all share the same breath . . .
>
> This we know. The earth does not belong to man: man belongs to the earth. This we know. All things are connected like the blood which unites one family. All things are connected.
>
> Whatever befalls the earth befalls the sons of the earth. Man did not weave the web of life; he is merely a strand in it.
>
> Whatever he does to the web, he does to himself . . .
>
> The white man too shall pass; perhaps sooner than all other tribes. Continue to contaminate your beds, and you will one night suffocate in your own waste.

I would much prefer to think that rather than suffocating in our own waste we will decide consciously to choose to understand the 'web of life' and the role we play within it. It's not going to be easy! Knowing that old habits die hard makes me very aware of the difficult pathway ahead. But on the other hand, I think that in our willingness to protect the earth the reward will be great, for our children will someday inherit the earth in all its mystery and wonder. Let it be so.

Janus

The speaker elaborates on the usual statistics:
weapons, famine and so on and so earnestly forth,
to students glad to skip chemistry and physics.

They soon forget how much exam grades are worth
as the litmus paper of their hidden fear
dips beneath the surface of her facts and figures.

The crooked globe stands alone at the rear,
expelled to the dunce's corner,
declining from them all into the wall.

Out of time, she assures everyone they can still
help right everything as a set of pupils
pour over the photograph of a Chernobyl

calf with two heads, wondering if the head
looking forward is the one living or dead.
   Greg Delanty

Glossary

The definitions and explanations given here are sometimes simplified or incomplete. More rigorous definitions can be found in technical source books.

Absorbed dose. The amount of radiation energy absorbed in a unit of mass of an organ or living thing from ionizing radiation.

Alpha particle. An electrically charged (+) particle emitted from the nucleus of some radioactive chemicals, e.g. plutonium. It contains two protons and two neutrons, and is the hardest of the atomic particles emitted by radioactive chemicals. It can cause ionization. Alpha particles are relatively heavy and large and cannot easily penetrate clothing or skin, but they are highly dangerous if inhaled or ingested. See 'Ionizing radiation'.

Atom. The smallest particle of matter that can take part in a chemical reaction. Some atoms may combine to form larger but still tiny molecules.

Background radiation. This includes emissions from radioactive chemicals which occur naturally and those which result from the nuclear fission process. The meaning of this term is vague. In a licensing process it includes radiation from all sources other than the particular nuclear facility being licensed, even if the source includes a second nuclear facility located on the same site (US regulation). Radioactive chemicals released from a nuclear power plant are called 'background' after one year.

Beta emitter. A nuclide which releases beta radiation.

159

Beta particle. An electrically charged (-) particle emitted from some radioactive chemicals. It has the mass of an electron. Krypton-85, emitted from nuclear power plants, is a strong beta emitter. Beta particles can penetrate a centimetre or more of living tissue but can be stopped by thin sheets of denser materials. They can also cause ionization. See 'Ionizing radiation'.

Chernobyl AIDS. Radiation-induced Aids which breaks down the immune system.

Dose. Energy imparted to matter by nuclear transformations (radioactivity). This is the general term for the quantity of radiation absorbed by the body.

Dosemeter (sometimes spelt 'dosimeter'). A device used to measure doses of ionizing radiation.

Electron. A negatively charged atomic particle that is lighter than protons and neutrons. All atoms are made up in part of electrons. A free electron is one which is not associated with a nucleus.

Element. A substance which consists only of atoms of the same atomic number and which cannot be split up into simpler substances by chemical means. There are over 100 different elements, of which 92 occur naturally.

Fallout. Radioactive materials which descend from the atmosphere onto the surface of the earth. Fallout may be caused by nuclear explosions, by the release of radioactive substances after a nuclear accident, and by the routine operation of nuclear facilities.

Gamma rays. Electromagnetic radiation of high energy and penetration released by some nuclear transformations. They are similar to X-rays and will penetrate through the human body. Iodine-131 emits gamma rays. Both gamma rays and X-rays cause ionization. See 'Ionizing radiation'.

Gene. A unit of heredity composed of DNA, occupying a fixed position on a chromosome. A gene may determine a characteristic of an individual or regulate or repress the operation of other genes.

Genetic effects of radiation. Those effects which are experienced by the children of the individual receiving the radiation or by later generations – in contrast to somatic effects, which occur in the individual receiving the radiation, and teratogenic effects, which occur in the embryo or foetus inside the mother's womb.

Graphite. A soft form of carbon used as a moderator in nuclear reactors.

Half-life, biological. The time required for the body to eliminate one half of an administered dose of a radioactive chemical. It is influenced by health and diet. The main methods of elimination are via urine, faeces, exhalation and perspiration.

Half-life, physical or radioactive. The time taken for the activity of a radionuclide to lose half its value by decay. The chemical resulting from the transformation may be either radioactive or non-radioactive. The process of radioactive decay is independent of temperature, pressure or chemical condition. Half-lives range from less than a millionth of a second to millions of years. The half-life is a characteristic constant for each particular nuclide. An individual nuclide may decay before or after the half-life. Radiation is released every time a radioactive material changes to the next material in its decay series.

Radioactivity per unit weight is inversely proportional to the half-life. For example, a specified quantity of caesium-137 (half-life 30.04 years) is about 76,000 times more radioactive than the same quantity of caesium-135 (half-life 3 million years). Iodine-131 is a radio-isotope with a half-life of eight days.

In traditional nuclear physics there is a rule of thumb that after ten half-lives a substance is considered to have decayed to a 'safe' level. However, this rule does not consider the size of original quantity of the radioactive nuclide, nor is there a universally accepted definition of what is 'safe'.

Hot spot. A local geographic area where radioactive environmental contamination levels are higher than average for the surrounding area. Hot spots may be a tiny point containing only a few radioactive fragments, or they may encompass many square kilometres, such as when an air mass or cloud containing a high concentration of radioactive dust becomes part of rain or snow. Areas of body tissue where a much higher than average concentration of radioactivity occurs are also referred to as hot spots.

Ionization. This occurs when sufficient energy is deposited in a neutral molecule to displace an electron, thus replacing the neutral molecule with positive and negative ions.

Ionizing radiation. Radiation with enough energy to ionize atoms, i.e. to remove electrons from them. It includes X-rays and gamma rays and the particles that are emitted from radioactive substances. High levels of ionizing radiation can have noticeable, severe and lethal effects on the human body. At low levels, none of our senses can detect ionizing radiation. We cannot see it, hear it, feel it or smell it. However, although we are unable to detect it with our senses, damage to the human body can occur which only becomes apparent years later. Radioactive nuclides pose the greatest threat to human health when they are inhaled or ingested. However, radiation-emitting fragments can be so small that they fasten in the many sweat pores and hair follicles all over the body.

There are three main types of ionizing radiation: alpha, beta and gamma. Alpha emitters are the most harmful to living cells if ingested or inhaled, but the distance which alpha particles can travel is only a few centimetres in air and mere tens of microns in soft tissue. Beta particles can travel up to about 80 centimetres in air and they cannot go through steel or wood thicker than about one centimetre.

The difference between alpha and beta particles is like that between cannon-balls and bullets. Alpha particles, like cannon-balls, have less penetrating power but more impact. For this reason the biological damage of alpha radiation is considered to be about 20 times that of the same absorbed dose of beta or gamma radiation.

Gamma rays are a type of electromagnetic radiation, unlike alpha and beta radiation, which are forms of particle radiation. Gamma radiation can be as harmful as beta radiation and can travel great distances. The majority of gamma radiation is stopped by a few centimetres of concrete.

When discussing the distance which different forms of radiation are capable of travelling, it is important to distinguish between radioactive particles and radioactive emitters. Alpha and beta particles travel a very short distance, due to radioactive decay. In contrast, minute dust fragments containing alpha, beta and gamma emitters can be transported great distances by wind and water. Sometimes the false impression is given that locations only centimetres away from a radioactive source are isolated from exposure. See also 'Alpha particle', 'Beta particle' and 'Gamma ray'.

Isotope. One of two or more forms of an element that have differing atomic weights, i.e. that have the same number of protons but different numbers of neutrons. It is considered that after ten half-lives a radioactive isotope has decayed into another radioactive isotope (a daughter product) or has become stable. See 'Radioactivity'.

Low-level radiation. This includes background radiation and man-made radiation from low-level nuclear waste. The International Commission of Radiological Protection assesses radiation damage on the premise that radiation is always potentially harmful, however small the dose.

Natural background radiation. Low-level radiation from space and from radioisotopes in rock, soil and building materials. It includes emissions from radioactive chemicals which are not man-made. These chemicals include uranium, radon, potassium and other trace elements. They are made more hazardous through human activities such as mining and milling, since this makes them more available for uptake in food, air and water.

Neutron. A neutral elementary particle. In the nucleus of an atom it is stable, but when free it decays.

Plutonium. A man-made highly toxic synthetic metallic element with a half-life of 24,400 years. Traces of plutonium occur in uranium ore and it is produced in a nuclear reactor by neutron bombardment of uranium-238. The isotope plutonium-239 readily undergoes fission and is used as a reactor fuel in nuclear power stations and in nuclear weapons.

Plutonium is an extremely dangerous substance because of its radioactivity and the fact that when ingested as an oxide or other compound it deposits in the bone and is excreted very slowly. Metallic plutonium is not absorbed by digestive organs. Inhalation of only a few thousandths of a gram may lead to death within a few years and much smaller quantities can cause lung cancer after a latent period of about 20 years.

Plutonium should be handled by remote control using extreme caution to avoid the release of dusts to the atmosphere. Plutonium metal is highly reactive and thus must be stored at low temperatures in dry air to avoid corrosion. It was first identified in experiments at the University of California in 1940, and plutonium-239 was isolated a year later. There are 16 isotopes of plutonium, of which only five are produced in significant quantities: plutonium-238, -239, -240, -241, -242.

Proton. A stable, positively charged particle in an atomic nucleus.

Rad. The old unit of absorbed dose of ionizing radiation. One rad is equal to 1 rem for most forms of radiation. The rad was first defined in 1953. In 1956 the rad replaced the roentgen (a unit of radiation exposure) for clinical work involving X-rays or radioactive sources. In practice the rad and the roentgen both represent about the same amount of energy, since 1,000 rad equals 1,050–1,150 roentgens, but unlike the roentgen, the rad is applicable to all types of radiation. Historically, the rad can be traced back to 1918, when it was suggested as the name for the unit of X-ray dose sufficient to kill a mouse.

Radiation. The emission and propagation of energy through space or tissue in the form of waves. This term usually refers to electromagnetic radiation, classified by its frequency: radio, infrared, visible, ultraviolet, X-rays, gamma rays and cosmic rays.

Radioactivity. The emission of radiation from atomic nuclei.

Nuclear radiation includes alpha and beta particles, gamma rays, X-rays and neutrons.

Rem. The acronym for roentgen-equivalent-man. This unit of dose equivalent was replaced by the sievert.

Sievert. The international unit of dose equivalent. One sievert is equal to 100 rems.

Somatic effects of radiation. Those effects which are experienced by the individual receiving the radiation – in contrast to genetic effects, which occur in offspring or future generations, and teratogenic effects, which occur in the embryo or foetus inside the mother's womb.

Strontium-90. A radio-isotope with a half-life of 28.2 years. It is one of the hazards of fallout.

Teratogenic effects of radiation. Those effects which are experienced by the embryo or foetus inside the mother's womb – in contrast to genetic effects, which occur in children of the individual receiving the radiation or in later generations, and somatic effects, which occur in the individual receiving the radiation.

Uranium. The heaviest naturally occurring element. This dark grey, radioactive, metallic element was discovered by the German chemist H.M. Klaproth in 1789. Uranium is both radiologically and chemically toxic and poses a health hazard as a heavy metal as well as a radioisotope. Uranium-235 is used as a source of nuclear energy by fission.

GUIDE TO RADIO-ISOTOPES

Isotope	Radiation	Half-life	Organs affected
Americium-241	alpha	433 years	blood and bones
Barium-140	beta & gamma	13 days	bones, reproductive organs
Caesium-137	beta & gamma	30 years	muscles, reproductive organs
Carbon-14	beta	5,600 years	bones
Cobalt-60	beta & gamma	5 years	liver
Cobalt-60	gamma	5 years	reproductive organs
Iodine-131	beta & gamma	8 days	reproductive organs, thyroid
Krypton-85	beta & gamma	10 years	reproductive organs
Krypton-95	beta & gamma	10 years	lungs
Phosphorus-32	beta	14 days	bones
Plutonium-239	alpha	24,400 years	blood, bones, lungs, reproductive organs
Plutonium-240	alpha	6,600 years	blood and bones
Polonium-210	alpha	138 days	spleen
Potassium-42	beta & gamma	12 hours	muscle, reproductive organs
Promethium-137	beta	2 years	bones
Radium-266	alpha	1,620 years	bones
Radon-222	alpha	3.8 days	lungs
Ruthenium-106	beta & gamma	1 year	reproductive organs
Strontium-90	beta	28 years	bones

Sources of information

Reactor Accident Report (World Health Organisation, 6th May 1986).

CORE (Cumbrians opposed to a Radioactive Environment).

WISE (World Information Service on Energy, Netherlands).

No Immediate Danger, Dr Rosalie Bertell, 1985, The Womans Press Limited, London.

Beyond Chernobyl: Women Respond, compiled by Corin Fairburn Bass and Janet Kenny, 1993, Envirobook, Sydney, Australia.

Index

Chernobyl Children's Project

By the end of 1995, the Chernobyl Children's Project had delivered $4.25 million of medical and educational aid to hospitals and children's homes in Belarus and had brought more than 1000 children to Ireland for recuperative holidays.

In January 1995 the first English branch of the Project was launched in Manchester. During its first year it sent two ambulances and a 38 ton truck of aid to Belarus, and hosted its first group of 38 children for a holiday in the Greater Manchester countryside. Further branches have now been established in Lancaster, Merseyside, South Lakeland, Northumberland and Wales. Many more children will visit in 1996.

If you have been moved by this book and would like to do something to help the children of Chernobyl, please contact either of the following:

Chernobyl Children's Project
8 Sidneyville
Bellevue Park
St Luke's
Cork
Republic of Ireland

Tel: 021 506411

Chernobyl Children's Project (UK)
One World Centre
6 Mount Street
Manchester
M2 5NZ

Tel: 0161 834 8176

The Ethical Investor
How to make money work for society and the environment as well as for yourself

Russell Sparkes

Growing interest in the morality of business activity and in environmental issues has led to a rapid increase in ethical investment. Businesses, such as the Co-operative Bank, are attracting high-quality custom by investing only in this way.

In *The Ethical Investor* Russell Sparkes illustrates how ethical investment empowers people in a practical way. They may choose to benefit the causes important to them, including women's rights, rain forests, the status of workers in the Third World or alternative technologies. They may equally choose not to support businesses which care only for profit and not for the harmful consequences of their exploits. The book shows how ethical investors forced change on South Africa, and how they are currently fighting for the environment.

Packed with up-to-the-minute information and statistics, *The Ethical Investor* is an essential handbook for anyone who wishes to invest – either by creating their own portfolio or choosing a fund – and retain a clear conscience over how their money is used.

'…packed with information and comment…a thoughtful book by a practising Christian who knows his subject and has done extensive research to present the details of ethical investment to a wide band of readers in a fascinating and objective way.'
Church of England Newspaper

Witness
A Holocaust Memoir
Samuel Drix

'*Rich in detail and insight ... it brilliantly describes the colourful life of pre-war Lwow's Jews and uncovers the darkness surrounding their brutal death at the Janowska camp. Read it and you will not regret it.*' Elie Wiesel, author of *Night* and winner of the Nobel Peace Prize

When the German Army captured Lwow in 1941, Poland's third largest city contained a vibrant Jewish community of 160,000 people. It was one of the first areas to be subjected to the Nazis' "Final Solution" and its Jewish population came close to complete eradication. Mainly because so few lived through this persecution, it is a very poorly recorded aspect of the Holocaust.

Samuel Drix, a respected Lwow doctor, survived, but he lost every member of his large family, including his wife and two-year-old daughter, and almost all of his friends. He endured nearly a year in the infamous Janowska concentration camp, helping fellow prisoners to stay alive. Miraculously he escaped, and hid with a Polish farm couple until the Red Army arrived and the war ended.

Nazi anti-Semitism was replaced by the Russian kind. A broken man, Drix contemplated suicide until a woman's love gave him renewed hope. His story is a powerful and moving addition to Holocaust literature.

Russian Resurrection

Strength in suffering –
A History of Russia's Evangelical Church

Michael Rowe

In this authoritative and fascinating volume, Michael Rowe traces the rich but troubled history of evangelical Christianity in Russia and Ukraine, from pre-revolutionary times through to the present post-Communist regimes. Vividly brought to life by many personal accounts and stories of individual Christians and congregations who have risen above the seemingly endless tide of persecution, *Russian Resurrection* is a thrilling and inspirational record of the perseverance of faith and hope, and essential reading for all concerned about the future of the persecuted Church.

Michael Rowe is a freelance Russian translator and researcher who has previously worked for Keston College.

'A veritable flood of factual detail from scattered sources has been channelled into a well-integrated account.'
Baptist Quarterly

Love Letters From Cell 92

Dietrich Bonhoeffer and Maria von Wedemeyer

Dietrich Bonhoeffer, the German Christian thinker, was arrested in April 1943 for conspiring to assassinate Hitler. He had been engaged to eighteen-year-old Maria von Wedemeyer for just two weeks.

The story of Dietrich and Maria is told through their letters, withheld from publication until now. Despite their difference in age and background, their physical separation and the censorship of their letters, an intense love developed between them during Dietrich's imprisonment. It is an inspiring and uplifting story, but ultimately tragic, as Bonhoeffer was to die at the hands of the executioner in April 1945. Their hopes for the future were never to be fulfilled.

'I've chalked a line around my bed,' Maria wrote, 'roughly the size of your cell. You have a table and a chair in there, the way I picture it, and when I sit there I almost believe I'm with you. If only I were...'

'Their letters...are revealed in *Love Letters From Cell 92* to be luminous with a belief in the value of love, in the sublime no less than the passionate sense (but how much a kiss meant!)' Frederic Raphael, *The Sunday Times*

The American Jew

Dan & Lavinia Cohn-Sherbok

The American Jewish community is more influential than ever before. Who are these individuals? Do they speak with one voice? How have they become so rich and powerful? What do their non-Jewish neighbours feel about them?

American rabbi Dan Cohn-Sherbok and his wife Lavinia spent four months in a typical Mid-Western city finding the answers to these questions. More than one hundred people speak for themselves, from the Orthodox rabbi to the teenage summer camper, from the self-made millionaire to the doting grandmother, from the Auschwitz survivor to the eighteen-year-old débutante.

Their stories are as gripping as the best fiction and, at the same time, provide a unique snapshot of American Jewry in the 1990s.

Trial and Error
Mordechai Vanunu and Israel's Nuclear Bomb
Tom Gilling and John McKnight

Mordechai Vanunu worked as a technician at Israel's top-secret Dimona nuclear research complex for nine years before being dismissed in 1985 for pro-Arab sympathies. He left Israel on a journey that finished in Sydney, Australia, where he became friends with a clergyman, John McKnight. As a result of his conversion to Christianity, he decided to expose Israel's clandestine activities.

Retaliation was swift and ruthless. Vanunu was kidnapped by Mossad agents and tried behind the closed doors of a Jerusalem courtroom. Convicted for espionage, treason and betraying State secrets, he was sentenced to 18 years in jail. Despite being nominated for a Nobel Peace Prize, and having his case taken up by the European Parliament, Vanunu's appeals against the sentence have been rejected, and he remains in solitary confinement, forbidden to speak even to the priest who brings him communion.

A royalty on each sale of this book will be given to support the fight for his release.